Productivity

What They Should Have Taught You in School About Goal Setting, Time Management, Self-Discipline, Procrastination, Habits, and Mental Toughness

© Copyright 2020

This document is geared towards providing exact and reliable information regarding the topic and issue covered. The publication is sold with the idea that the publisher is not required to render accounting, officially permitted, or otherwise, qualified services. If advice is necessary, legal or professional, a practiced individual in the profession should be ordered.

From a Declaration of Principles which was accepted and approved equally by a Committee of the American Bar Association and a Committee of Publishers and Associations.

In no way is it legal to reproduce, duplicate, or transmit any part of this document in either electronic means or in printed format. Recording of this publication is strictly prohibited and any storage of this document is not allowed unless with written permission from the publisher. All rights reserved.

The information provided herein is stated to be truthful and consistent, in that any liability, in terms of inattention or otherwise, by any usage or abuse of any policies, processes, or directions contained within is the solitary and utter responsibility of the recipient reader. Under no circumstances will any legal responsibility or blame be held against the publisher for any reparation, damages, or monetary loss due to the information herein, either directly or indirectly.

Respective authors own all copyrights not held by the publisher.

The information herein is offered for informational purposes solely and is universal as so. The presentation of the information is without contract or any type of guarantee assurance.

The trademarks that are used are without any consent, and the publication of the trademark is without permission or backing by the trademark owner. All trademarks and brands within this book are for clarifying purposes only and are owned by the owners themselves, not affiliated with this document.

Contents

INTRODUCTION 1
CHAPTER ONE: PRODUCTIVITY AND WHY YOU LACK IT 4
    WHAT PRODUCTIVITY IS 4
    THE OPPOSITE OF PRODUCTIVITY 5
    YOUR DEFINITION OF PRODUCTIVITY 5
    WHY YOU LACK PRODUCTIVITY 6
    LET'S TALK ABOUT LAZINESS 7
    PROCRASTINATION VS. LAZINESS 7
    A LITTLE ON IDLENESS 8
    WHY YOU GET LAZY 9
    WHY YOU PROCRASTINATE 10
CHAPTER TWO: PROCRASTINATION IS JUST A BAD HABIT 11
    DIVING DEEPER INTO THE DIFFERENCES BETWEEN LAZINESS AND PROCRASTINATION 12
    LAZINESS CAN BE YOUR FRIEND 13
    PROCRASTINATION; YOUR ANCHOR 13
    BREAKING THE HABIT OF PROCRASTINATION 14

- Understanding Habits 15
- An Edge over Procrastination 16

CHAPTER THREE: THE EFFECTS OF STRESS ON PRODUCTIVITY 19
- How Stress Affects You 20
- Stress and Your Productivity Levels 20
- The Damage Stress Causes You 21
- How to Live a Stress-Free Life 22
- When You Don't Have Mental Space 25
- How to Properly Engage with Tasks for Less Stress 25
- Other Ways to Beat Stress 26

CHAPTER FOUR: MINDSET MATTERS – 13 STEPS TO CHANGING THE WAY YOU THINK 28
- Let's Get Real 28
- A Negative Mindset 29
- Changing Your Mindset and Behavior for the Better 32

CHAPTER FIVE: GOAL SETTING – MYTHS, TRICKS, AND PROVEN METHODS 36
- What is Goal Setting? 36
- Goal Setting and Productivity 37
- Myths about Goal Setting 38
- Proven Tricks and Strategies for Goal Setting 41

CHAPTER SIX: FINDING YOUR FOCUS AND STAYING FOCUSED 44
- Focus 45
- Sleep and Focus 45
- How to Stay Focused 46
- Distraction Steals Your Life 50
- Define Your Life's Mission 51
- Say No 52

CHAPTER SEVEN: TIME MANAGEMENT HACKS YOU NEED TO KNOW 53
- Same Time, Different Results 54

THE BENEFITS OF TIME MANAGEMENT	54
TIME MANAGEMENT AND PRODUCTIVITY	55
HOW TO BECOME A TIME MANAGEMENT GURU	56
YOU CAN BUY EVERYTHING BUT TIME	57

CHAPTER EIGHT: HUSTLE CULTURE – THE BIG DOS AND DON'TS .60

WHAT HUSTLE CULTURE IS	61
A BATTLE AGAINST STEREOTYPES	62
THE GOOD THING ABOUT HUSTLE CULTURE	62
HOW SOCIAL MEDIA FUELS EXTREME HUSTLE CULTURE	62
DON'T BUY INTO THE HYPE	63
WORKAHOLISM AND TOXIC PRODUCTIVITY	64
THE GRIND WILL GRIND YOU	65
WORK/LIFE BALANCE	66
HEALTHY HUSTLE	66
WHY YOU SHOULD HUSTLE THE RIGHT WAY	67
HUSTLE CULTURE DO'S	67
HUSTLE CULTURE DON'TS	69

CHAPTER NINE: 10 STEPS TO SELF-DISCIPLINE .70

ARE YOU SELF-DISCIPLINED?	70
TRUE SELF DISCIPLINE	71
THE CURE FOR LAZINESS AND PROCRASTINATION	71
A SELF-DISCIPLINED TURTLE	72
WHY PEOPLE AREN'T SELF-DISCIPLINED	72
KNOW YOUR LIMITS	73
SELF-DISCIPLINE AND PRODUCTIVITY	73
HOW TO BE SELF-DISCIPLINED	74
WHAT TO EXPECT AS YOU DISCIPLINE YOURSELF	75
DOING WHAT YOU LOVE VERSUS LOVING THE PROCESS	76
STEPS TO DEVELOP SELF-DISCIPLINE	76

CHAPTER TEN: HOW TO CULTIVATE MENTAL TOUGHNESS .81

    Mental Toughness Isn't Just for Sport 82
    What Mental Toughness is All About 82
    The Benefits of Acquiring Mental Toughness 83
    Mental Toughness and Productivity 84
    How to Build Your Mental Toughness 85

CHAPTER ELEVEN: THE ROAD TO SUCCESS – 25 STRATEGIES FOR GROWTH 88
    What Success Is 88
    A Success Mindset 89
    Three Keys to the Success Mindset 89
    How to Develop a Success Mindset 90

CHAPTER TWELVE: FORMING GOOD HABITS THAT LAST 92
    Myths about Building Habits 93
    Micro Targets, and Macro Goals 93
    On Plans, Triggers, and Changes in Behavior 94
    Habits You Should Practice Daily to Stay Productive 95

CONCLUSION 98

REFERENCES 101

Introduction

There are a lot of books that have been written about productivity by people who know next to nothing about it. They pretend that they're masters of productivity. You'd believe it too when you look at the list of achievements they carry around and are ever so happy to brandish every chance they get. Given enough time and observation, you come to realize that they're nothing more than skilled advertisers. They'd do very well in the world of Mad Men, assuming they were a product that needed marketing.

This book is different. It's not enough for me to just write that. I invite you to go through this book, page by page, with a fine-tooth comb if you will, and you'll notice that you're getting a lot of gold from it. Here's a little something about gold: It can change your life for the better — if you're smart about how you use it.

People have all sorts of views on what productivity is. For some people, it's able to complete their book or create a business. For others, it's about committing to a workout program each day and striving to be better. A trader would consider their day productive if their trades hit their take profit levels, and they're in profit at the end of their day. An artist could find their productivity in learning one more way that their artwork does or doesn't work. Same for the scientist. Productivity could also mean being able to spend time with family and friends, building your relationships.

What I'm trying to say is that productivity is all about the various ways in which you try to put your time, energy, money, and smarts to good use, so that you can get the best reward possible, without killing yourself. Productivity is a journey. On this journey, you learn how to achieve results without having to suffer dire consequences.

In this book, you're going to learn what productivity entails. You'll be able to peek under the hood and see just how it works. The insight you'll gain from reading this will help you finally understand why some folks are more productive than others.

The fact that you're reading this book tells me two things: One, you want to become a better version of yourself, and two, you are all too familiar with procrastination. You've probably resigned yourself to a lifelong sentence in procrastination prison since nothing all the books out there suggest seems to work for you. Well, good news! You're going to learn how to tackle procrastination once and for all. You will also learn the best time management skills you need so that you can not only be more productive but also eliminate stress in your life.

What productivity really all comes down to is self-discipline. You must master yourself if you're going to make the most out of each day in your life. But I'm sure you're wondering, "How can I master myself? What's the first step?" This book will dive into that as well. Here's a hint though: A big part of self-mastery comes from changing your mindset, or as I prefer to call it, your state of mind. Once you do that, then all your actions have no choice but to come from that state of mind. I assume the state you desire is that of productivity. Why else would you be reading this?

There's a misconception floating around that productivity is all about working harder, and for longer, until you exhaust yourself. It's not about making things more difficult so that it can be easier to achieve stuff. There's no logic in that! What productivity really is about is what you choose, moment to moment. It's about how you choose to think about yourself. It's about how you choose to make decisions. It's about making choices. Each of these choices inevitably moves you closer to or further from your goal. There's no stagnancy. You're always on the move.

My goal by the end of this book is to give you all the tools you need to start moving in the direction of your dreams and aspirations. By the end of this book, you will find that you have a keen eye for choices that advance your productivity. You will learn how to make your life phenomenal — using the least amount of effort. In other words, you will learn what true productivity is all about.

Chapter One: Productivity and Why You Lack It

How do you define productivity? Typically, productivity is all about the proper measurement of efficiency. In other words, it's about being able to figure out how to get the most milk from one simple squeeze. Now, let's make this more relatable and personal. How can you determine how productive you are in your day to day affairs? After all, chances are you don't have a cow, and even if you did, the bulk of your life is not about just getting milk out of it.

What Productivity Is

Put simply; productivity is all about getting optimal results for very little effort and time. The reason you're reading this book is that you're on the hunt for ways that you can make the most of your life, and achieve all that you've set out to do while giving yourself all the leeway you need to focus on stuff that matters to you.

The Opposite of Productivity

Picture a successful, handsomely paid employee of a Fortune 500 company. He wakes up 6 AM in the morning, gets ready for work, and is in there by 7. From the minute he walks into the building, it's *go time*. He's on the phone with business partners in Istanbul for an hour. Right after that, he jumps right into another meeting with potential clients, and after a couple of hours, he's landed them. Now he needs to get back to work on a proposal that he needs to have ready in the next three hours — and this is only one of seven deadlines he must somehow beat today! It sounds like a very busy dude! Sounds productive, doesn't he?

Well, this is not productivity. It's not about being busy all day. It's not about doing one task after another, trying to beat deadlines, and constantly taking on more and more duties. Never assume that being busy equals productivity. In truth, when you're productive, life does not feel like you're forever under pressure. You don't feel like you're behind. You get a lot more done with a lot less effort! True productivity is about learning how to make the most of the 24 hours we all get each day. It's about making sure that in all your drive to achieve, you also feel fulfilled. It's smart about work. Hard work doesn't pay off in today's world. Smart work does.

Your Definition of Productivity

Just like anyone else who is interested in being more productive, you want to have more time so you can devote that time to the stuff you care about. You know, the stuff you could do endlessly without pay because you're too busy enjoying yourself. When you can hit your targets on time, this means that you will be able to do other things. The upside of increasing your productivity levels is that you'll be a lot less stressed in life. That's worth it in my book.

Now, do not misunderstand me; I'm not saying that you should make a list of stuff to do and then check them off as you achieve them. Quite frankly, unless you enjoy what you're doing, that's boring, and could easily lead to you being burnt out. Productivity means passion is in the picture, as well.

Why You Lack Productivity

Why have you chosen the goals that you have? Take a moment to really think about that. It matters that you deeply consider why you want to become a more productive person. Knowing your why will make it easier for you to become the version of yourself you'd rather be. So, is your desire to increase your income? Would you like to move to a new, better home? Is it that you want to spend more time with family and friends? Or would you simply like more time to learn a new skill, or travel the world? Figure out what it is that's driving you to want to be better. Once you know what your why is, then it becomes easier for you to stay on track, even on the days when it feels like all you want to do is be an unproductive slob. If you had a reason in sight of being more productive, then you would find it easier to keep up with your goals.

Another reason you're not as productive as you would like to be is that you probably don't have role models, or you don't have the right ones, anyway. So, once you know what productivity means to you, then you simply need to look around you and spot someone you can emulate; this must be someone who is the very essence of who you'd like to become in your life. Success has a formula. The way to find it is to look at those who are already the very person you see yourself becoming, and then copy them. There is no need to reinvent the wheel. It also helps to look at those who aren't doing so great when it comes to being productive. Why? This way, you can clearly see what not to do, and avoid or curb any similar habits you might have in your own life.

Let's Talk About Laziness

Alright, I'm not going to coddle you. If there's something you're supposed to be doing, but you're not doing it because it seems way too difficult or "stressful," then quite simply, you are lazy. I'm not trying to make you feel like crap. I'm simply stating the facts, which, deep down, you know to be true. You may have observed that rather than do what you need to do properly, you only get to work as a matter of necessity. There's no spark, no passion whatsoever. Either that, or you choose to do something else entirely because you find "something else" to be more interesting, and less of a pain in your derriere. Or, even worse, you simply do nothing. To cut a long story into itty bitty bits, you're lazy if you are more inclined to save your energy, rather than motivated to do what you need to. Simply put, laziness is all about avoiding pain or trouble.

Procrastination vs. Laziness

Let me make this clear: Laziness and procrastination are two peas in two different pods, each on opposite sides of the universe. When you procrastinate, you simply choose to delay doing what you know needs to be done by doing other stuff that's easier to handle, or more fun for you. These things are often not as important as whatever it is that has you dragging your feet.

With that said, just because you must postpone something for reasons that are constructive or inevitable does not mean you're procrastinating. You are procrastinating when you're postponing stuff because you haven't planned properly, and as a result, you're going to pay a hefty price for it. That price could be avoidable expenses, guilt, stress, or sheer unproductivity.

The one thing that procrastination and laziness do have in common is that there is zero motivation. Your procrastinating self-

differs from your lazy self in that you do plan to finish the task at hand, and more often than not, you do finish — even though it means you have to deal with a lot of headaches in the process since you wasted precious time.

A Little on Idleness

When you're idle, you're doing nothing. Sometimes, it's because you have nothing to do. Or, it could be that you do have the stuff to do, but now, you can't do it because there's something in the way. Or, you just finished working on a project, and you're taking a break. Or, wait for it, you're lazy.

Ask the average working woman or man why they work, and they'll tell you something that comes down to this: To get more free time. For many, what drives them to get to work is their desire to be idle. The funny thing is, it's pretty hard for us as humans to remain idle. Don't believe me? The next time you go to the DMV, take a good look at everyone queuing up and tell me whether they face saying, "Ah, standing here, doing nothing. Such bliss."

I'm not just saying no one likes to be idle. Science backs me up on this, too. There's research that shows even though we seem to value being idle a lot, we will often find a reason to get busy, no matter how silly it is. In fact, a lot of people are happy when they're busy, whether it's them or someone else giving them the stuff to do. People often set goals for themselves simply because they get to stay busy. Why, though? Well, a lot of people aren't particularly okay with being idle, because their minds go places they'd rather not visit. So, it's just easier to stay busy and distract themselves.

With that said, there is such a thing as productive idleness. Basically, you choose to take time to deliberately do nothing. There are prominent men and women who do this and attribute much of their success to this deliberate idleness.

Why You Get Lazy

If you're going to beat your laziness and be more productive, then you need to understand what it is that keeps you lazy. You see, back in the days of caves and clubs, our ancestors had to be smart about the way they expended energy. They had to save their strength so that when needed, they could flee from predators or fight. The game of the day was survival. This meant long term goals were not on the agenda.

These days, survival is not quite as important, since we have better medicine, better ways to eat, better roads, and stuff that generally makes life easier. Add in the fact that we have better life expectancies, and it becomes obvious that one must think about the long haul. Obvious as that may be, the reason you're still lazy and focused on the short term like our ancestors, is that you're still hardwired to save your strength! The last thing you want to do is start that screenplay you've been talking about or set up that new e-commerce store. Who's to say it will all be worth it anyway? You'd rather put your time, energy, and money into stuff that will pay off right this minute. You're fluent in the language of instant gratification.

Now, there's a chance you're not actually lazy, even though it seems like it. It's possible you simply haven't found something you would love to do, or you know what you'd like to do, but you just can't do it now. It could also be that you work a very abstract job that doesn't allow you to fully appreciate the value you bring to others, in the way a surgeon can see how she has made someone's life better, or a movie producer can see how they've touched others through film.

You might also find that you're plagued by a constant feeling of hopelessness, and a fear of success. You don't feel comfortable doing well for yourself, so you get lazy, because that's a surefire way to sabotage yourself. Or, it could be that you're afraid to fail. How can you fail if you don't try, right? Better to not bother, you think to yourself.

It could be that you're lazy because you assume that your life or circumstances are practically hopeless. You can't quite figure out how you could change anything. If this is the case, then it's not necessarily that you're lazy, it's that you feel the circumstances you're in are so unforgiving and unbending that you don't even have the luxury of choosing to be lazy.

Why You Procrastinate

What is it about us that makes us so willing to delay stuff we know we should take care of, even though we know that delay is going to cost us big time? Sometimes, it's a matter of being a perfectionist. You could be so particular about getting stuff done right, that you never do anything at all because you worry it won't work out well. Sometimes, you con yourself into thinking you're making headway, by buying and studying everything you can about whatever you need to do... but, in reality, you know more than enough and should just take the plunge and get busy on the task!

You might also have a fear of the unknown. You know what needs to be done, you're just not sure what the results might be, and you're afraid that they will hurt you, or your efforts will have been for nothing in the end.

You also procrastinate because you keep thinking you can always get "a round tuit" later. It would help if you realized there is no such thing as a "round tuit" and that you should probably get to work now. When you suppose that the right time to do the job will come along in a matter of hours or days, you will create a lot of stress for yourself. You erroneously assume when the time comes, you will have all the energy you need to get it done. What you don't realize is there's every chance when the deadline draws near, you'll have zero inspiration, zero motivation, and other obligations screaming for your attention as well.

Chapter Two: Procrastination is Just a Bad Habit

Like me, I'm sure you know what it's like when there's a deadline dangerously close, and yet for some reason, you just can't find it in you to get your tasks done. You'd rather spend the bulk of your time checking out memes on Reddit or watching the latest show Netflix suggested for you. You could decide to focus on other stuff that isn't urgent. In fact, the very thought of watching a kettle of water boil sounds even more interesting than whatever it is that you're procrastinating on.

You might also be very familiar with the feeling of simply wanting to meditate, by which I mean you become one with the couch, snacking on stuff that's bad for your waistline and your health in general. You may have found yourself spending days, even weeks, busy doing a whole lot of nothing.

Diving Deeper into the Differences between Laziness and Procrastination

The first paragraph was all about procrastination, while the second was about laziness. I touched on the difference between the two just a little bit in chapter one, but I really want to get into it now. The last thing we need is to give you a cop-out like, "I'm not lazy, I'm just procrastinating," when in fact, you're lazy, or vice versa.

Procrastination, simply put, is a bad habit. When you constantly keep delaying stuff you should do - especially when it's important or urgent - you're procrastinating. When you're lazy, it just means you don't really feel like doing any work at all, not anything. Laziness is indolence, which is a word that, interestingly enough, comes from the Latin word "indolentia." Indolentia means "without pain or trouble." Procrastination is from the Latin, pro crastinus, which means "belonging to tomorrow."

The procrastinator feels a lot of guilt about deliberately putting off work, especially when they know that if they don't do it now, it will mean disastrous consequences. Procrastinating is not the same as deliberately scheduling something for later. When you schedule, you're following a plan and managing your time. Procrastinating is when you've decided to write that thesis that's due in 5 days, but you realize now's a good time to clean the house. You know it would be in your best interest to do what you need to do now, but you choose to do something else entirely.

Now that you know the etymology of both words, you should have a clue how these two are totally different things. When it comes to procrastination, you're not avoiding work. You simply postpone it until you can no longer delay it while you work on other things that are not as important. When it comes to laziness, you're making an effort to make no effort at all. Only, it's not effort. It seems to be the easiest thing to do.

Laziness Can Be Your Friend

It's not necessarily a terrible thing to feel lazy. In fact, often, it's your mind's way of telling you that you need to take a moment; otherwise, you're going to burn out. You need to give your body and mind some time to recuperate if you plan to operate at peak performance in your tasks. Some people recover overnight, some in a week, some a bit longer. Where the problem sets in is if you let this laziness steadily eat away at your months and years. Next thing you know, you're in your 80s wondering where the heck you went wrong. In this case, it could be a symptom that something is wrong psychologically, and it's not about your need to recuperate.

Procrastination; Your Anchor

You're not the first person to have to deal with procrastination, and you won't be the last. Heck, sometimes, I find myself feeling tempted to do just that! The thing about being a procrastinator is that life passes you by as you keep delaying what you should do. Therefore, it is vital that you learn to kick this habit by replacing it with good ones. You simply must take your life back!

People don't think procrastination is that bad, but the truth is this is one of the biggest things that keeps you from becoming the best version of yourself, whether it's in relationships, or in business, or whatever, really. What people wind up regretting the most is not the stuff that they have already done, regardless of the outcome, but the stuff they never did or haven't done yet.

Procrastination steals your peace of mind, as you're riddled with guilt over not doing what you should do, and regret because your constant delaying has allowed some excellent opportunities for growth to pass you by. Whenever you procrastinate, you're basically wasting time. This is time you'll never get back; the time you could have spent doing something that would benefit you in the long run. Once you can cut yourself loose from the anchor that is procrastination, you will find yourself soaring in life, and you will accomplish more than the average person in today's age.

Now, I don't want you beating yourself up over all the times you've procrastinated in the past. There's just no sense in doing that. What you need to focus on is the now, and how you can finally learn to act immediately, without dragging your feet.

Breaking the Habit of Procrastination

Perhaps the first thing to do if you want to become that person who does things when due is to stop defining yourself as a procrastinator. I am not asking you to fake it until you make it or anything like that. I am simply saying, you have a habit of procrastinating. The great thing about habits is that you can make them, and you can break them as well.

You can break the habit of procrastination! You just need a little bit of science. See, it's easy to assume that the only reason you're procrastinating is because of the task you must do. However, it has nothing to do with what you've got to do. It's really all about relieving the stress you feel!

You may have some troublesome stuff going on in your life, like bad investments, trouble in your love life, the passing of a loved one, or other factors. Now, when you get to work, deep down inside, you're just a tense ball of stress, whether or not you choose to acknowledge it, and you realize that you have a lot to do for the day. You're well aware that some of it is really urgent and important, while some of it isn't. You know you've been focused on stuff that doesn't matter as much as the big projects you should be working on.

When you finally do sit down and decide it's time to take on those gargantuan tasks, your mind begins to panic. Your brain is not quite ready to deal with anything major, because, now, you're feeling very stressed out. You feel so stressed out that it tells you to look up some YouTube video your buddy had sent you the other day, and now, two hours have gone by, you're convinced that the earth is flat and that there are aliens living in the earth's core. Then you look at the time, notice you've not done anything at all, and then bam! The guilt hits you with a sucker punch to the gut!

Understanding Habits

How do you break this habit of procrastinating? There are three parts to habits:

- **The trigger.** When it comes to procrastination, the trigger you're dealing with is stress.
- **The repeated pattern.** In procrastination, the pattern is to avoid acting.
- **The reward.** The reward you get from the habit of procrastinating is stress relief.

There is only one way for you to break this nasty habit. No, it's not about eliminating the triggers, because there will always be one thing or another to stress you out, till the day you breathe your last. The way to break the habit is to change the pattern. That's it. Whenever you find yourself procrastinating, spending too much time looking at cat videos, or whatever here's what you must do:

1. Recognize that you're stressed. Acknowledge that there must be stressing you out right now.
2. Do a mental countdown. Count 5, 4, 3, 2, 1. When you do this, countdown, step three naturally follows.
3. Interrupt the habit of procrastinating. When you count down, you're basically doing what is called a "pattern interrupt." Also, you'll awaken your prefrontal cortex, which is the part of the brain that's responsible for self-regulation. This way, you stand a higher chance of doing what needs to be done.

4. Do some work for just five minutes. Set up a timer and get to work. Just pick one of the important, urgent things you've got to do, and then tell yourself it's only going to be for five minutes.

You're probably wondering, "How in the heck am I going to finish this whole project with just five minutes of work?" Well, what you'll find is that, interestingly enough, your problem is not having to work. Your problem is the constant habit of avoiding work. When you choose to work for just five minutes, a funny thing happens: You keep going. Research has shown that if you could only start, there's an 80 percent chance that you're going to keep going.

An Edge over Procrastination

Here are other ways you can make sure you always win in the battle against procrastination:

1. Pick just one thing. Sometimes, the stress you feel is not necessarily from some event in your life, but from the sheer overwhelm that comes from handling big projects with lots of moving parts to them. When you have way too much on your plate, begin by picking just one thing that you've been delaying, and then commit to it alone. Forget about the other stuff until you're done with it. Taking small bites like this will help you get over the stress, and make you believe your work is easier than you had assumed.

2. Begin NOW. Now that you know what you'll be doing, you just have to hop to it immediately. I've already shared with you how to get started. Just tell yourself it will only take five minutes, and then start. Remember, if you start, you're more than likely going to finish. This is on account of something known as the Zeigarnik effect, which is that if you've got something you're not done with, then it's likely you're going to keep thinking about it. All you need is five minutes.

3. Chunk up your work time. You could take an hour, where you decide you will concentrate on the work at hand. If an hour seems like it's a bit much, then you could try working at intervals of 20 to 30

minutes each, with 10 to 15 minutes of rest in between the work intervals. This way, your brain will perform at optimal levels, and you'll find yourself busting through work like it's nothing! The reason you should work in intervals is that research has shown that our brains are basically wired to have peak moments, as well as valleys. So, it makes sense to work with your brain so that it can give you all the best, and you don't feel like you're burning out.

4. Be kind to yourself. If you're going to beat procrastination, then you've got to be able and willing to forgive yourself for all the times you procrastinated in the past, especially if it cost you some missed opportunities. If you keep dwelling, you'll probably keep procrastinating, since you'll be stuck in a defeatist attitude of "There's no use, I might as well keep on trucking." Forgive yourself, and more likely than not, you will be able to stop procrastination in its tracks and do something.

5. Use music. There's that one song that gets you really fired up. Find it. Maybe there's even more than one. Maybe it's a whole genre. Find it and play it whenever you are about to get to work on something you've been dilly-dallying over. This way, your brain learns a trigger for your new, proactive habit, and more likely than not, you'll get to work, and you will see it through because the music feels so good.

6. Recognize why you're procrastinating. Like I've already mentioned, it's not about the work most of the time. It's probably something else that's stressing you out. If you can't figure out what it is, then it's probably about the sheer size of the work. You might feel overwhelmed. Once you know what it is you're afraid of or worried about, you're already halfway towards tackling the problem.

7. Release it. There's a chance that you have way too much on your plate, and it's time to let some of it go. You may have given yourself way too many obligations, or let people pile them on you. Either way, you need to go over that to-do list and see what it is you know you'll never even bother doing. Then cross it out. It's okay to release it.

There's only so much time and energy to do stuff. Channel them where they need to go, and scrape everything else off that plate.

8. Make a bet with a friend. This one is incredibly helpful. It's great to have someone who can keep you accountable. You can make a bet to have finished a certain project by a very specific day. Tell your friend or relative or colleague that if you haven't finished by then, you'll give them $20, or you'll treat them to lunch for a week or something. Then, they'll check in on you at the set time, and you either finished what you're doing, or you're going to spend your money buying them bagels and coffee for a week. Make a habit of this, and you'll never be tempted to procrastinate again! You can't keep your word either, because that makes you a waffle. No one wants to be a waffle.

9. Have fun with this. If you're finding it difficult to finish your work or to start, then you should make it fun. I have a friend who always has a special bottle of red wine chilling in the wine cooler. She never touches it unless and until she's done with whatever project she's working on. Maybe you could treat yourself by buying new clothes, or going to some nice place for dinner, every time you finish something you've been procrastinating on. This way, your brain learns to anticipate the reward and will do everything it can to help you bulldoze your procrastination tendencies and create better habits that serve you. Therefore, *think about ways you can reward yourself for getting stuff done.*

Chapter Three: The Effects of Stress on Productivity

In today's world, stress is a major problem. It makes it hard for you to be productive or make rational decisions. Science has found that stress, like alcohol, kills your brain cells, making it really tough for you to have clarity of thought. You may have noticed that when something is stressing you out, you have an urge to just throw your hands in the air and scream, "I quit," not just when it comes to the stressor, but in other things in your life as well.

I've already mentioned before that you're never going to be able to get rid of stress completely in your life. However, it helps to know how to deal with stress. It doesn't have to completely ruin your brain or your life, but it will if you don't manage it. Stress has a very detrimental effect on your productivity levels. Since this book is all about becoming more productive, then stress is worth looking into.

How Stress Affects You

You could be badly affected by stress right now and not even know it. If you're finding it incredibly difficult to fall asleep, or you're the victim of constant headaches or even worse, migraines, then you might be stressed. When you're stressed out, your body, mind, and emotions are all affected. It's important to know the signs to look out for that can let you know if you're feeling stressed. You may think this is not a big deal. After all, everyone is stressed these days, right? Well, stress can cause a lot of problems for you down the road. Besides dwindling productivity, you might also be a prime candidate for heart disease, high blood pressure, diabetes, and obesity! Talk about the gift that keeps on giving. Let's look at the different ways stress can affect you.

1. Physically, you might notice you have chest pain, an upset stomach, issues with sleep, constant fatigue, headaches and/or migraines, muscle pain and tension, and a drastic change in your sex drive.

2. Emotionally, you feel restless. You are low on focus and have zero motivation. You feel overwhelmed. There could be some anxiety, a persistent feeling of sadness, and depression. You find that every little thing makes you snap because you're so irritable and angry all the time.

3. Behaviorally, you might find yourself eating way too much or way too little. You may resort to the use of tobacco or other drugs as a coping mechanism. Socially, you're withdrawn. You're prone to fits of anger. You drink more and exercise way less.

Stress and Your Productivity Levels

A 2010 study in the International Journal of Productivity and Performance Management by George Halkos and Dimitrios Bousinakis, was carried out with the goal of learning how stress and job satisfaction affect the way a company functions. The study focused on factors like a good working relationship between employees and management, the number of work hours, the productivity of the group, and the connection between the worker's education and the work they do. For this study, 425 workers in both the public and private sectors were enlisted.

What the study revealed was that when the workers were stressed, their productivity levels plummeted. When they were satisfied, those same levels skyrocketed. Whenever the employee's work lives began to spill over onto their personal lives, then the overall impact on productivity was alarmingly negative. This just proves the point that you've got to get a better handle on your stress levels in life if you want to be more productive.

The Damage Stress Causes You

There are so many horrible things that happen when you are stressed out:

- Zero time management. You may be completely terrible at managing your time. The result is that you often find you have way too many deadlines looming in the too-close horizon. Now, stress has some advantages, in that when you're stressed, you've got the adrenalin flowing through your system, and you're more motivated to take care of those tasks that you need to handle. With that said, when you have no support from your peers, way too many obligations, and a workload heavier than Everest, then there's a problem. You begin to panic. You're frustrated because you don't think you have all the time you need to not just finish the work but finish well. You find that you've got to start working from home and putting in extra hours. That's no fun for anyone.

- Issues with your social and romantic life. Your friendships and relationships are not safe from stress, either. You might find that you're constantly worn out — too worn out to bother with the people that matter in your life. You find that you no longer interact as freely as you used to with your significant other, your family, friends, and colleagues, as well as being unable to focus. You feel overcome by hopelessness, and you're completely helpless. Also, for some reason, you can detect criticism, even when it's not there. You feel resentful, paranoid about everything, and probably struggle with depression as well. All these things take an inevitable toll on your social life.

- Zero focus. When you're stressed out, you just can't focus. You could morph into a cat-like Professor McGonagal from Harry Potter, and someone could turn on a laser beam and have it right in front of you, but you still would not be able to focus. This lack of focus caused by stress makes it really tough for you to learn new things and apply what you've learned. Constantly contending with tension, anxiety, and worry on account of a stressful life, makes it all too easy for you to be distracted, and make mistakes which range from benign to disastrous.

- Compromised health. Stress really does a number on your body. You can't sleep right; you can't think through the brain fog or the headaches that constantly attack you, you can't eat because it's sure to cause you problems, and you just hurt all over your body. Naturally, when you feel like crap, whatever work you do will suffer for it. The solution might be to take a break so you can recuperate from these stress-related illnesses, but what happens when you get back? You've got a backlog of work to deal with, and you're back to being stressed out again.

How to Live a Stress-Free Life

The weird thing about situations that cause us to feel stressed is that there's always a certain stillness in the eye of that mad, raging storm. However, it's not easy for everyone to find it. When you do find it, though, the sense of calm you get is undeniable. The reason you can feel that calm is because, at the moment, you're in a state of mind that allows you to act in a way that is productive and positive. You're in the zone at that moment. This means you follow your intuition when you make critical decisions about this storm raging all around you. In the process of making decisions, you find that you are engaged in a meaningful way to achieve a certain result.

In that moment of calm, all the unimportant stuff fades into the background. The chatter in your mind dies out, and you're fully in the here and now. It's a peaceful feeling. Now, imagine a situation where you don't need to be in a situation of crisis before you can tap into that sense of calm and peace. Is it possible? Definitely.

What's stressing you out is not that you haven't done what needs to be done, but that you are thinking about this the wrong way. You are not engaging with what's happening in the right way. This is very central to beating stress.

I'm talking about proper engagement. Take a moment to consider why you need some sort of life or death crisis to get you to that point of full engagement in the present. Here's your answer: Crisis often forces us to do the things that cause us to get to that point.

To beat stress, you simply must properly engage with whatever it is you're working on, whether it's a project, or more time with your dog, or better health. Just take a moment and notice what's going on in your mind. What else is cooking in your noodle, besides reading this book? Here's why that question matters: The more you think about it, the more it's not actually happening, and the more you are improperly engaged with it. You're still mulling things over because you're trying to figure out what needs to be done or still trying to find out how to make the results you've gotten so far to work for you.

When you find yourself stressed, you don't need to get a new planner, or start a new to-do list, or get some fancy time management app. Those are great and all, but in the end, they're just tools. You need certain principles in order to fashion a system that works for you, a system that has you properly engaging with the task at hand, rather than being stuck in your head, overthinking instead of acting.

I should also warn you that when you put these principles into practice, they will feel very unnatural in the beginning. You'll feel awkward. You might even argue with yourself, thinking "none of this crap is necessary!" It's not unlike in Karate Kid, where he must chop wood and carry water, and it all seems very irrelevant to the actual skill of fighting. However, the more you practice, the more you'll notice you're doing better, and you'll see the positive effects spill over into other areas of your life. This is what some of the stuff I'll be sharing with you will look like.

Now, when you've got a project that will need several steps before you can finally complete it, you must become clear on the results you expect, and what the project is about. Once you're clear, go ahead and put that on your list of projects, and once or twice a week, look at it. Take every single action you will have to take to make your project happen, and make it clear on the list so that you can see it often.

I understand that all of this will feel very unnecessary, but these little things will give you the ability to be spontaneous about getting to work on your dreams. This is the key to success.

You're probably wondering where I'm going with this, and why any of it matters. The crux of the matter is that in times when you're not dealing with any obvious, immediate crisis, there is still some crisis happening beneath the surface, especially since you can now focus on other things out there in the world that you previously didn't bother with when you were dealing with a crisis that was immediate and apparent. Now, you're swamped with all kinds of things that you should do, or could do, or need to do, or might do. It's piling up all around you, from possible meetings to emails to phone calls, etc. Given enough time, it all comes into your mind, and makes you feel overwhelmed, conflicted, confused, and stressed out. The usual reaction to this state of mind is to either grow completely numb and lazy or get incredibly busy. When you choose to be busy, you get stressed. Then you assume the stress is because you don't have enough time. However, time is not the problem here!

What's the problem then, you wonder. It's simple: Mental space. You could have all the time in the world, but if you don't have the mental space to process your projects, you still will accomplish next to nothing. You don't need time to be creative. Creative ideas can occur to you in an instant, as an inspiration. It's not about time. It's about the mental space to have the creative energy, so that you can engage properly with your tasks, in the here and now, without feeling stress or burnout.

When You Don't Have Mental Space

When, like most people, your head is full of clutter that could be organized into systems, it makes it hard for you not to feel stressed out. Things get messy — and not in a good, creative way. When you have room to be creatively messy, come up with ideas, go off the script, you find that you're incredibly productive. However, when your mental space is cluttered with such basic things as reminders and details like that, then you don't have the room to be productive. You notice your lack of productivity, and you feel even more stressed out because you're wondering what the hell is wrong with you. You need that space because you can't have a pool party when your pool is cluttered with dead leaves. You must clear that pool.

If you're going to beat stress, think about the way your life at home and at work are, right now. Can you keep trucking the way you are over the long haul? Do you find you're unable to take advantage of creative ideas and opportunities as they come to you? If your answers are no and no, then you've got to change a few things.

How to Properly Engage with Tasks for Less Stress

First, grab a notepad and a pen, and write down every idea that crosses your mind over the course of a day. The idea is not to think the same thing twice. It doesn't matter whether it's about your personal life or your work life. Big or small, write it down. AS you do this, you will notice your mind is a lot less cluttered with thoughts about what you should be doing and is more engaged with whatever it is you are doing.

Next, get clear on your outcomes. You need to be certain of what you need to do. It's not enough to have a to-do list. Make it clear what the outcome you expect from doing this task is. It's the difference between writing "dog" on your to-do list, versus "walk the dog," or "feed the dog."

Other Ways to Beat Stress

1. Know the signs of stress. It's important that you know what happens to you when you're stressed, so you can better manage yourself.

2. Talk with your loved ones. It's important to have a support system that can help you make changes you need to so you can reduce your stress levels.

3. Figure out your triggers. Once you know the stuff that makes you stressed out, then you can become more creative in how you deal with them if you can't help but do so, or in avoiding them as best as you can.

4. Workout. When you work out, your endorphin levels rise. The cortisol level in your body plummets, you feel better and less stressed. It doesn't have to be intense. Just move your body!

5. Practice mindfulness. I can think of no better way to keep you properly engaged in the here and now than to practice mindfulness. There are all sorts of mindfulness techniques, from mindful breathing to mindful walking. See what works best for you.

6. Get a good night's sleep. When you don't sleep long enough or well enough, you will be stressed out. Make sure you get at least 7 hours each night and be regular about when you go to bed and when

you wake up. Before you sleep, don't do any cardio workouts. Stay away from caffeine, and don't eat in the hours leading up to bed.

Chapter Four: Mindset Matters — 13 Steps to Changing the Way You Think

The thing about procrastination and laziness is that it all comes down to your mindset. In fact, I'd go so far as saying the state of affairs in your life right now reflects what your state of mind has been. If you don't like it, the first step is not to change what you've been doing, but to change your state of mind. When you transition to the state of mind that your ideal version of yourself would have, then taking the actions needed to be more productive becomes easier, and everything you do in order to achieve that is a lot more effective.

Let's Get Real

I'd like you to ask yourself some questions. Be honest with yourself.
- Do you find that your revenue or productivity at work is dwindling?
- Are you always worried about clients possibly leaving you?

- Do you bend over backward to do everything your client wants, even to your own detriment?
- Does it seem like no matter how much time and effort you put into your projects, you just don't see your workload lightening up at all?
- Do you constantly wake up and go to bed feeling defeated and stressed out?

If you answered yes to all these questions, then you have got to make some changes, starting now. You've got to look at what's happening in your mind, so you know what needs to go and what needs to stay, for you to have the proper, productive mindset. Whenever you notice stagnancy in your life, an inability to focus, and a lack of drive, then it's time to check out your mindset and fix it.

A Negative Mindset

When you decide to do something, it can be hard to stick with it. This is especially the case where it's something that completely falls to you and no one else. In times like this, it's easy to get negative. If you let your mindset become a negative one, then you will find that you're constantly moving from bad situations to even worse ones. You can't focus. You can't think creatively. You have the energy for nada, and so nada is what you do. So, what are these negative mindsets that hold you back from achieving your greatest potential?

- **Feelings of inadequacy.** If you find that you're always beating up on yourself, no matter how many clients you've made happy, or how much effort you have put into your projects, then you have the wrong mindset. You can't expect to be a winner in life when deep down inside, you feel like you keep losing, and you'll never be good enough.

The fix: Do you feel like you really are good enough. A great way to do this is to look back on previous successful ventures, so you can feel confident about your abilities. Don't just look back, though. Look ahead as well. Don't settle and assume that your current output is all you're capable of. Know that there's always room for improvement. When you become lackadaisical about your work, your colleagues, bosses, and clients will notice. They, too, will become that way to you, and you become dispensable.

- **Feelings of hopelessness.** In life, you've just got to have some metal for you. Otherwise, you will find that you're always defeated before you even start the game. Or, if you have one little mistake or failure, you just throw up your hands and quit. If this sounds like you, then this is a terrible mindset, you need to change right away.

The fix: Don't be too quick to accept defeat. Also, make peace with failures and mistakes. There's nothing wrong with failing because it's all part of the process of success. Suck it up, knowing that mistakes always teach you more, and failures help you get better. Don't let them chip away at your drive.

- **Impatience and desperation.** This is not a good vibe at all, in any aspect of life. Do you find that you're always impatient with the pace at which your work is going? Are you frustrated because things are not happening as quickly as you'd like? Well, then you'd better watch out! This feeling of impatience can lead to you, making some terrible choices that will not work out well for you in the long run. It could hurt your project, or whatever business it is you're running.

The fix: Recognize that good things take time. Sure, sometimes, what you want can happen fast. However, learn to be like a patient crocodile, waiting for its prey to swim to it before it snaps its jaws shut. Only ever make decisions and act when you're feeling stable and in no rush.

- **Feelings of helplessness.** When you start something new, you are the one who is responsible for whether it flies or dies. You might think this responsibility is a bit much for you to bear, and as such, you're overwhelmed by feelings of helplessness. Don't be.

The fix: Recognize that just like riding a bike, these are things that will feel natural to you over time; don't sweat it too much. Think back to all the times you started something new and were uncertain, and yet were able to make it work. This new project or business you've got going is no different from those times.

- **Overwhelmed by fear.** The thing about fear is that you're choosing to believe in a terrible turn of events that, for all intents and purposes, is not real. It has not played out yet. If you find that you're always giving in to your fearful thoughts, then you're either going to be completely paralyzed and unable to move forward with your goals, or you'll be taking all the wrong decisions from a place of fear.

The fix: Understand the worst that could happen, and then gently remind yourself that it would not be the end of the world. Then go ahead and do whatever it is you need to in order to be more productive.

- **Shame.** Shame can be a terrible thing when you choose to wallow in it. When you make mistakes, do you find yourself constantly rehashing them in your head, to the point where you can't even think of a way forward? Then you must change that mindset.

The fix: Understand that crap happens. Get over it. There's no such thing as perfect, and you'll never be it. Focus on the way forward, rather than wallowing in the past.

- **Underwhelm.** Do you find that you're completely unsatisfied with the quality of your work? Are you bored, perhaps? Do you wonder every so often if you're even in the right field? You are plagued by feelings of dissatisfaction. Sometimes, what you do may feel totally underwhelming. There's no challenge. If all your neurons except two went on vacation, you'd be able to do what you do easily. You don't feel like you're growing at all. You hate it, but you've grown comfortable. It's time to shake things up.

If you're always dragging your feet in the morning or looking for any chance to hop on to something new because it's a lot more fun than what you've been doing, then you're due for a mental tune-up.

The fix: Know that you always have the option to make changes. You don't have to stay stuck where you are. As that profound saying goes, "Move. You are not a tree." Even trees spread out their roots and branches! Get a picture of what your dream day would be like, and then make plans and take action to make it happen.

• **Overwhelm.** This is a common one, especially when you're self-employed. You might feel like you have an impossible workload. You feel like you're completely out of control, and constantly having to dance to other people's tunes.

The fix: Recognize your personal signs of burnout. Be willing to admit that you may have pushed a little too hard, and you're in need of a break. Also, be honest with yourself about whether you're adequately compensated, and then work towards fixing that.

Other mindsets that don't work for you are feeling like you're unproductive, disorganized, and must do things on your own instead of delegate. Feelings of being broke, resentful, guilty, and alone also do not help in any way at all. So how do you change your mindset, exactly?

Changing Your Mindset and Behavior for the Better

1. Begin anew. Each day is a new one. So, start new. Forget about what went wrong yesterday, and just carry on with your day. Take ten minutes at the start of your day to just sit, shut your eyes, and observe your breath. Make sure you don't reach for your cellphone or check your email for the first 30 minutes after you wake up. Take some time to think about the things you're most thankful for in your life. Also, think about three things you'd love to be very successful at or three things you'd love to experience in the future. Try to get some exercise in, even if all you can manage is 10 minutes. Then you can reset from the negativity of the previous day.

2. Clear your workspace. Make it somewhere you're more than happy to sit at. Keep it organized, so you don't feel stressed out

wondering where what is. When your workspace is organized, it's much easier for you to feel productive and creative.

3. Have your own safe spaces. When you're going to work, have a space that is just for that and nothing else. This tells your brain that every time you enter the room, it's time to get going, and you must be productive. When you experience bad stuff like a deal gone bad, leave your workspace, and go somewhere else to process those feelings. Don't bring the negativity into your workspace. It should be a safe space for you to create.

4. Systemize everything. You want to make sure you have consistency in your work life. This means you must create systems that will allow your work to flow with no hiccups and give you the mental space we talked about earlier. Look for ways that you can streamline the more mundane, repetitive operations so that you don't start to procrastinate or get lazy about doing the important stuff.

5. Structure your day. When you give your day some structure, you will notice that you're a lot more productive all day. Assign chunks of time to various tasks and learn to move on to the next thing with no hesitation. When you set up your daily structure, you must honor yourself by honoring it as well. This way, you are guaranteed to achieve a lot more in your day.

6. Do the stuff that sucks first. Find the most difficult task you must accomplish, and then get that out of the way. When you do the stuff you dread the most first, then everything else that comes up the rest of the day is like a cakewalk. Also, the boost you get from having achieved something so monumental at the start of your day will drive you to smash through the rest of your goals with ease and flow.

7. Never multitask. There's nothing cool about multitasking. Every task suffers for it. It's best for you to have a laser focus on one thing, knock it out of the park, and then move on to the next. The time you're checking your emails is for just that. The time for a set meeting is for that meeting, and not the time to be fiddling with your phone. Be mindful. Don't multitask. Remember, if you're going to be

productive, then you must learn to properly engage with the task you're working on.

8. Acknowledge that you can't do everything. It's exhausting for you to do everything. In fact, you can't. That's why smart, productive people delegate. Know your strengths and focus on them. Delegate the things you need done that you're not so great at, and/or do not have the time or energy to handle yourself.

9. Never take on projects you cannot complete or cannot handle. The same thing goes for projects that you're way better than. Don't work because you're desperate for cash when you know for a fact that you could be getting a lot more money for your trouble. Also, don't take jobs you know next to anything about, because if you do a bang-up job, then your confidence takes a critical hit, and that can affect the way you do subsequent jobs.

10. Be at peace with failure. Again, you're not perfect. Perfect does not exist. That is completely okay. I'm not saying you should use that as a cop-out when you botch things. Own your mistakes and your failures. Just don't beat yourself up about it, when you could use that time and energy to move on to better solutions. Figure out why whatever went wrong happened, learn your lesson, and keep it in mind as you move on.

11. Always celebrate your wins. Don't let anyone make you feel like something is too small or insignificant. Celebrate! No matter how little.

12. Make a point of learning every day. This is how you stay sharp. This is how you prevent the feeling of underwhelming, or boredom from creeping in. When you learn and apply what you learn, you grow in not just knowledge and skill, but value as well. This means you get paid the big bucks because you're not settling for the status quo. Look out for masterclasses, webinars, seminars, and books about your area of expertise, so you can learn more each day.

13. Get a support system. You're never going to make it on your own. Relationships are important. Have a network of people who are friends, family, or just folks in the same field as you are so that you

feel a sense of community, and support. These are absolutely vital for increased productivity and success.

Chapter Five: Goal Setting — Myths, Tricks, and Proven Methods

What is Goal Setting?

Goal setting is key to productivity. It is the process of figuring out the outcomes you want out of life in general, so that you have a solid framework to work off of, and you actually make progress. A lot of people are just like driftwood, floating, going nowhere exactly, even if on the surface you can see that they're working really hard to make something of themselves. For the most part, they have no set destination. Does this sound like you? Well, if it is, we're going to have to fix that by setting some goals the right way. When you've properly set your goals, you're going to find yourself being naturally productive.

Goal Setting and Productivity

The 80/20 rule or the Pareto Principle states that there's a natural division of people in society into two distinct groups, when it comes to how much influence and money they have:
- The Trivial Many. Or the bottom 80 percent.
- The Vital Few. Or the top 20 percent.

All things in the economy are subject to this same principle, where 80 percent of the country's wealth is actually controlled by 20 percent of its population. Now, you can actually apply this same 80/20 rule in almost anything in life, including goal setting and productivity.

In applying the Pareto Principle to goal setting, 80 percent of your results are determined by 20 percent of your activities. In other words, if you have a list of 10 super urgent, important things to get to, then only 2 out of those 10 things will be worth a lot more than the remaining 8 altogether. It is a very sad state of affairs that, for the most part, people will place more importance on the trivial 8 rather than the vital 2, which would give them the success and productivity they seek.

If you want to apply the 80/20 rule to productivity and goal setting in your life, then you've got to do a few things:

1. Write down 10 goals. Once you're done, it's time to get real with yourself. Ask yourself, if there was only one thing you could make happen on that list, right here and now, which one would it be that would have the best impact on your life as a whole? This is vital because this is how you get successful. Ask yourself what the second most important goal is. Keep that in mind as well. Keep going with the questions, as you run through your list.

2. Work on your chosen goals all the time. Remember, it's not about being busy. Productivity is not about being all over the place, forever swamped, but accomplishing little to nothing. Save yourself the heartbreak by working on tasks that are of high value, and not procrastinating by taking on unimportant tasks. One aspect of tasks that bring you the most value: they're often the most complex, hardest

things to do. With that said, when you're done, the reward is worth it, and could completely turn your life around for the better. Before you get to work each day, figure out the tasks that are in the 80 percent realm of "not vital," and the ones that are in the 20 percent realm of "vital." Then pay attention only to the vital 20 percent of your tasks.

3. Forget about dealing with the little things first. Little things are not worth it, and you'll never be done with them because they pop up ten times a second! In the end, you'll have nothing to show for all your exhaustion when you focus on the little things instead of the big stuff. Sure, it's tempting to start simple, but don't do that. Always get the hard stuff out of the way first. Make that your brand-new habit, so you can continue to make progress.

There's a study that was recently carried out on goal setting, which investigated the difference in how poor and rich people go about setting their goals. The findings were interesting. One thing they noticed is that 85 percent of the rich have one huge goal that they're always working on. Meanwhile, only 3 percent of poor people have a huge goal; it's just that they never work on it much!

You obviously want to be productive. You want wealth. You want success. To get all of this, you must act as the wealthy do. Success and failure both leave clues behind. Look and study successful people, emulating their behavior. Pick one big thing and keep working on it. This is how you can change your life. Keep in mind that when you have very clear goals, you will always have the perfect answer to make them happen, when you need it. This is advice from the one and only Brian Tracy, so you know he knows what he's talking about.

Myths about Goal Setting

To make sure you don't set yourself up to fail, then you must know what myths you might believe about goal setting. You can have the very best of intentions if you've got the wrong idea about what goal setting is, then all the best intentions in the world will not help you become more productive. Let's look at the various myths about goal-setting you believe that could be setting you up to fall flat on your face.

1. I need SMART goals, and I'm golden! No, you're not. A lot of books and motivational speakers talk about making your goals SMART. You must have heard this before: Goals need to be Specific, Measurable, Attainable, Relevant, and Time-bound. Let me be the first to disabuse you of this notion right now. You see, I've noticed time and time again that it's this SMART thing that messes a lot of people up. There is no cookie-cutter recipe for setting goals.

Now, do not get me wrong. The SMART way works, but it's not the whole story. Think of it like a movie trailer, and not the whole movie. The problem with the SMART method is that it doesn't work all the time for every kind of goal, especially when you're talking about long term goals. It's easy to get demoralized after a while when you work with the SMART method.

Goals are as complex and distinct as the people who have them. AS such, whatever system you want to use to achieve your goals has to be flexible, of you're going to succeed with it.

2. Goal setting is pointless. What often inspires this thinking is the idea that you really cannot predict the future, and as such, you should not even bother setting goals. I get it. Really. However, there's a little something called "mental forecasting." Sometimes the weather person says it's going to be sunny all day, and then next thing you know, it's raining. Go figure. For the most part, you know you can trust the forecasts. This is the same thing we're talking about here.

It's understandable that there will be speed bumps along the way of achieving your goals, but when you set your goals the right way, you make room for the unpredictable stuff. Kind of like carrying an umbrella just in case of a shower. Setting your goals the right way will give you the tools you need to keep going, especially when things happen that make you want to quit or make you stressed out. This is just one more reason that the SMART method is not so smart.

3. I've set goals before. It didn't work. Never will. It's fascinating that some people think this way. It's like, you fell in love, but it didn't

work out, and so there's no such thing as love, you say. There are a number of reasons why goal setting may not have worked for you. It could be a matter of the circumstances or the timing of things. Or, you could have chosen a goal setting method that just doesn't work for you. Or you set your goals the wrong way. None of this automatically means goal setting doesn't work for you. All you need is to learn from your previous attempts so that you do not repeat the same behaviors that lead to your failure.

4. Systems matter more than goals. The funny thing about this myth is that goals and systems are actually two peas in a pod. They're two sides of a coin. You can't have one without the other. When you set a goal, you must take action. This is where your system comes to play. When you have a system, no matter how effective it is, if you have no goals, then there's really nothing to tell you whether or not you're being productive or being busy. Systems are the tools with which you can reach your set goals.

5. Not reaching goals makes you a failure. No, it doesn't. You need to adjust your mindset. That the goal was not accomplished might have nothing to do with you. The problem may actually lie with the method and tools you used to try making that goal a reality. Perhaps your product or service hasn't achieved the goal you've set, because there was a problem with your product design, or with the marketing.

You would do well to look at failure in a different light. Think of them as temporary setbacks. A setback is just that. You can take some time to reevaluate where you're at, where you're going, and how you're getting there. You can readjust your deadline and keep on going. Focus on the fact that you've made it so far and learn from what went wrong so you can keep going further.

6. There's no need to write down your goals. Actually, you do. When your goals are only in your head, then they won't be very clear. You won't be able to take exact actions. You'll just keep winging it. Unless you have a lot of dumb luck, winging it is not the way to achieve your goals.

You absolutely need to write them down and keep them visible. This way, everything you do is about your goal. You can see it. You can take time to reflect on it and see how you're doing. You can use it to inspire you to do more and be better. Write down your goals. This will improve your focus and make distractions powerless. You will automatically be a lot more productive with your goals staring you in the face.

Realize that when it comes to setting goals and smashing them, the process is a continuous, complex one that is definitely worth it. It's the way you make your dreams happen. You just need to make sure you do not buy into any of these myths, and that you have the right tools. Then, your goals are a go!

Proven Tricks and Strategies for Goal Setting

One of the people that comes to mind when I think about success and productivity is the great Tony Robbins. That is a man who knows how to set goals, and smashes them, and he's a great role model to have. Let's get into the strategies he suggests for making sure you achieve your goals, all the time.

1. The pursuit is just as important as the prize. A lot of people don't think about the other stuff that happens as you make your goals real. It's a journey that will change you forever in one way or another. When you work on your goals, you will change. However, to paraphrase Tony Robbins, the goal of a goal is not about getting it, but about the person, you become in the process. This growth is where the real success lies. This growth will show you that you're capable of so much more than you think you could achieve.

2. Have the right timeline in mind. If you set a goal to lose 50 pounds in a month, then unless you're going in for liposuction, let me be the first to heartily announce to you that you will fail hard and fail big. You need to keep your goals reasonable. Set goals that you know you can achieve within whatever time frame you have. If not, you will

find yourself constantly disappointed with your lack of progress and overwhelmed by how far you have to go. If your goal will take longer than a year, then it helps to set benchmarks by which you can measure your progress, so you're more inclined to keep going.

3. Focus on the wanted, not the unwanted. If your goal is centered on what you don't want, then you're not going to get far. What is it you do want? Don't say to yourself, "I don't want this beer gut." Think, "I want to be lean, fit, strong, and have a healthy BMI." The great Robbins has suggested that whenever you can't figure out what it is you want, then you need to *do* something. Take actual physical action. He suggests going for a run while focusing on what it is you want.

When you constantly think about what you don't want versus what you *do* want, you are operating from a fear-based mindset. Change your mindset. I've already shared how you can do that. Become the person who feels the fear, and still goes after their goal.

4. Keep going even after you've hit your target. So, you made a million dollars. Congratulations! Don't stop there, though. Always set new targets to reach. This is how you grow. If you don't have a new target, then you're quickly going to find yourself wallowing in fulfillment and depression. It won't matter how lofty the goal you hit is. If you're unfulfilled, then you have failed in the biggest and worst possible way.

I'm not suggesting you should not take some time to enjoy the fact that you've nailed your goal. By all means, do! You must celebrate. Just make sure you think about what else you want next, make that your new goal, and keep at it. This is the way to stay satisfied with your achievements in life. It's not the goal you want. It's the growth. This is why you have new ones with each one you check off your list.

5. Don't fret about nailing our goals. I know you're probably confused by this one. After all, isn't the reason for setting the goal... the goal? Well, then you might need to reread this section because you haven't been paying attention. The goal is not the goal. *Growth is the goal.*

The reason that we keep looking for what to do is that we feel the most alive when we're making progress. The journey, or the progress, is what matters. That's what life is all about. Growth means many things to many people. Figure out what it means for you and aim for that. Seek growth, and you will become the best version of yourself. When you do, you'll realize even then, there's always room to stretch some more. That's the beautiful thing about life.

Chapter Six: Finding Your Focus and Staying Focused

Do you find it really difficult to focus? Are you the sort of person who would rather multitask? Then you might need to read this chapter twice. Maybe thrice. For some reason, the first thing most people do when they say they want to be more productive is looking for the latest system or the most cutting edge tools that self-proclaimed expense swear up and down will have you so productive you'll make a million a month or something. Also, for some reason, no one ever wants to think about how their habits could be hindering them from being as accomplished as they'd like to be.

You need to understand that your productivity level comes down to the habits you have. It's really in your hands. You could have the very best systems to help you stay on track and organized, but the fact of the matter is sometimes, you just can't for the life of you to be productive. No matter how bad you want to. Sometimes, this lack of productivity can stretch over a period of days or weeks. When that happens, it all comes down to one thing: Focus.

The only way you can ever finish your daily goals is by actually staying focused on them long enough to finish. Focus matters a whole lot more than any organizational system or tricks in the book. I don't care if you have the latest ToDoList app on your phone, your laptop, and a tablet. You still need focus, or it's all for nothing.

Focus

The way to get things done is to properly engage with the task at hand. I know I've said this for the umpteenth time right now, but that's the truth, and I hope to ram it into your head so that it becomes your life mantra. You simply must be a master of your attention.

One of the interesting things about attention, or focus, especially when it comes to creative or intellectual tasks, is that it's precious. As in scarce. Also, it can and usually gets depleted. So, when you spend a lot of time focused on one activity, you need to give yourself a break so you can do other things that don't require such concentration. This way, you can recharge your focus levels, and get back in the game.

When you are unable to pay attention to the task at hand, the last thing you should do is keep going — unless you just feel like frustrating yourself, for some reason. What you should do is recharge. You do this by taking a break from whatever it is you're doing. Find what works for you like a break. For me, I take a walk or take a nap, or I just do something mindless like play Candy Crush or watch an episode or half an episode of a good show on Netflix. The latter might not work for everyone, but I've learned to cope with attention burnout by doing that, and it works for me. You could try to have a chat with someone, listen to some music, or meditate if you're into that.

Sleep and Focus

Sleep is so underrated, in our caffeinated world. You should get enough sleep, and it's got to be quality as well. When you don't sleep enough, your cortisol rises. You feel incredibly stressed out, and you're unable to do anything productive in your day. Sleep matters, because when you sleep, your focus battery is charged to the max. It's for this reason you need to focus on doing the complex stuff first thing in the morning, or whenever you wake up if you're a night owl. If you don't channel that focus, it will just waste away over the course of the day.

Coffee can be your friend if you use it within reason. If you use it as a tool to stay awake when you should be asleep, you are not doing yourself any favors. However, using it after a good night's sleep can do wonders for your productivity levels.

How to Stay Focused

If you would like to accomplish everything you've got planned for your day, day after day, then you've simply got to focus. There's no other way. So how can you focus? How can you make the most of your attention span?

1. Set reasonable targets for each day. Spread your targets or goals across the day, making sure it's clear what you need to do when. You could use an app to help you with this, or you could use a good old-fashioned pen and paper.

2. Set deadlines and honor them. I used to be a procrastinator extraordinaire until I learned the power of deadlines. It's important that you make sure the deadlines you set are reasonable, as you have more than enough time to do a good job. Make sure you always set deadlines in whatever you must do, and whoever you're dealing with, and you will find yourself crossing things off your to-do list so fast that the paper catches fire.

3. Break your tasks into manageable chunks. Feeling overwhelmed? It's natural to lose focus each time you think off the sheer amount of work you must do. The way to fix this and reclaim your focus is to chunk down the work into manageable bits you can

handle. You're going to finish a whole turkey one bite at a time. If you can swallow one whole, then you've got a problem.

4. Teach your mind to focus. We all have certain times of the day when we're extremely productive. What you should do is teach your brain to remain focused. It's possible to supercharge your focus past its usual limits. To do that, just decide that for two hours each day, you're going to work on your project, and you will entertain no interruptions and no distractions. When you make a habit of this, your brain gets used to it, and you're able to deliver quality on time, every time, no matter the task you're handling.

5. Chunk your time into bits. Some of those bits should be periods when you are not to be disturbed. You will take no calls, no meetings, no visitors, nothing during this period. Do you work from home? Then sequester yourself. Tell the family you will not be opening the door for anyone unless the house is on fire. When you compartmentalize your precious time this way, your brain learns to focus 100 percent on the task at hand and is not at any point interrupted by distractions.

6. Keep that cell phone away. I know you may think this is silly, or it's not that important, but you may not realize how much cellphones can ruin your productivity. Especially today, when a cell phone isn't just a cell phone anymore. Now you have a multiple notifications from Facebook, your email, Instagram, WhatsApp, and whatever other apps are out there. Your screen lights up, your phone gives alert after alert, and each time, you just cannot help but stop what you're doing and pay attention to it. Put your phone away! In the US alone, people are on their phones daily for five hours minimum. A solid 2.5 hours is spent messaging, social media, and looking at cat videos or playing games. Put your phone away, and you'll get back those five hours.

7. Quit multitasking. You can't compare the quality of work you put out when you're focused on a single task, versus when you're doing so many things at the same time. Look at your schedule for the day and sort every task out in order of importance. Then work on just

one thing at a time and watch how fast you move and how well you do.

8. Mindfulness is good. Practice being mindful. When you regularly do mindfulness meditation, you will be able to focus better, and you'll find it easier to learn and remember things as well. Besides boosting your focus, it does wonder for keeping you looking young and feeling at ease, even in terrible situations. Cool stuff, aye?

9. Understand your body's rhythms. Everybody has a clock. It's different for each person, which is why I still can't get over morning people and their need to judge the rest of us who stay up late and wake up later. In any case, you need to figure out your body's clock. Notice when you're the most productive and the time your most important work for that period each day.

10. 90-minute blocks are awesome. Learn to work for 90 minutes at a time. Why? There's a lot of research which now shows this is how we usually work, naturally. When you work in 90-minute blocks, you can focus. When 90 minutes have elapsed, you're going to have much slower action going on in your brain for 20 minutes. This is why you find it hard to focus at this point. So, work in 90-minute blocks and take a 20 to 30-minute break in between.

11. Give your mind a break. Mind breaks are the best boost you can give yourself when there's no coffee around. All you need is a little break, and you'll have a lot of inspiration and creativity pouring out of you. When you take that quick break, especially when you notice your mind is starting to get tired, you will feel refreshed and more inspired and motivated to continue with your work.

12. Use a timer. There's an amazing thing I discovered called the Pomodoro Technique, where you work on your task for 25 minutes, and then you take a quick break of 5 minutes, and then you get back to it for 25 minutes. Once you have done this cycle 4 times, then you get to take a longer break lasting 15 to 30 minutes. You can easily find Pomodoro timers online.

13. Get your exercise. Exercise is awesome, not just for the waistline, but for your brain as well. When you make a habit of

working out, you will notice that you're better at paying attention. Exercise helps you learn better, recall better, and focus like a laser. It also does wonders for your mood, making you feel like you're ready to take on the world once you're done.

14. Please declutter. I don't know how anyone could get any work done when they're surrounded by so much clutter. When you declutter, you create space not just on your desk, but in your mind as well. This allows creativity to flow, and allows you to focus, since there's nothing within sight or reach that could take your attention away from whatever you're doing. There is actual research that shows working with clutter in full view messes up your focus and productivity big time.

15. 2-minute magic. If there's something you must do that will only take a couple of minutes, *tops,* then do it right away. Don't save these little tasks; don't put them on a list, because that will just make you feel more overwhelmed. Just suck it up and do it. It will surprise you how much less stressed and more focused you get when you wrap up those little things in two minutes — preferably after you've handled your big thing of the day, of course.

16. Move to another task. Whenever you notice you're no longer focused on a task, and your mind feels like it keeps running up against a brick wall, then you should consider moving on to something else. This fresh change in scenery is sure to bring your focus back and keep you on track for longer. The result is that you'll be a lot more productive than you ever imagined you could be!

17. Make better food choices. When you eat right, you give your brain all the nutrition it needs to perform at its best, and this means you're going to be more productive at work. It's tough to focus when you have nothing in your stomach. With that said, do be mindful of how much you eat. Just because it's healthy doesn't mean you should overstuff yourself. So, eat just enough, but no more, otherwise you'll find you're too sleepy to continue with your work.

18. Use a DND Sign. A Do Not Disturb sign hanging right outside your door or by your workspace is more than enough to help your

colleagues and family understand that you're on the grind and need room to focus. Make sure that you let them know not to disturb you until a certain time, except in the case of an emergency. With some people, you might want to specify what you mean by emergency, or else they're going to just label every excuse to interrupt you as a matter of life or death.

19. Prepare for tomorrow. When you're done with your tasks for the day, take a bit of time to create your to-do list for tomorrow. Order them based on the 80/20 rule, so that you know what your day is going to look like, barring any surprises. This way, you come to work with a clear mind, knowing exactly what it is you want to do.

20. Refuse tasks. Or delegate. You're not superhuman. There are times when there will be far too much on your plate, and you just have to say no. If you know you don't have enough time, energy, or money to take on another project, then just say no. If it's something you cannot refuse for one reason or the other, then delegate. You might be worried about whether saying no will cost you a potential business relationship or future deals, but the fact is you can't just let people take advantage of your affinity for the word yes. Say no. And no, you don't have to explain.

Distraction Steals Your Life

You cannot afford not to be focused on your life. This is non-negotiable. Do everything within your power to increase your focus, so that you have a clear vision of your goals, and you have a higher chance of making them happen. It's up to you to decide to be focused. If you refuse to work on it, then guess what's going to happen? You're going to be destroyed by distraction.

You've heard the saying, "Opportunity comes but once." Maybe, for this reason, you've decided to say yes to everything that comes your way. Well, it's complete bull crap. I'll give you that one for free. You create your own opportunities. You have the right to say no to people and their once-in-a-lifetime opportunities. You don't have to do what everyone asks of you. If you keep doing that, one day, you're going to feel like a huge chunk of your life has been stolen by these distractions. You're going to feel like you have wasted your years, and you have nothing to show for them. You'll feel like you're doing work you don't give a crap about, and that you've allowed your relationships to slip away.

You must learn to develop a focus on your priorities in life. This is the only way you can have a quality life that you'll look back on with satisfaction in your sunset years. If you're going to take back your focus, then you simply must stop making so many decisions. When you keep making decisions, your brain eventually becomes worn out, because you're using up all the energy that could be used for willpower or making better decisions than all the ones we just allow ourselves to make. Stop making so many decisions! Stop spending all your time surfing the internet, and you'll notice you're no longer wasting energy multitasking, but focusing. Get off Twitter. Get of IG, Reddit, or whatever social media it is that has you focused on so many things that make your mind must keep deciding whether to click or not click.

Define Your Life's Mission

Have your overall mission for life and set your intention for each day. When you know what your mission for the day is, you can finally hone your focus, excluding everything that does not add to your mission or push you further down your path. If you're guilty of taking on too many projects, it's probably because you have not set your mission for life up. Now I'm not asking you to volunteer or help. However, when you spread yourself too thin, you lose focus, and you never become the person you want to be or do the things that you want to do.

If you don't have your own plans, someone is going to plan your life for you. You need to become proactive about your life's mission. Don't let your inbox dictate to you what you should do with your day. If you do, then you won't focus, and you will not make any progress. Ironically, as you progress, the more you focus on whatever you're progressing on. Figure out your mission, craft your days around it, and watch your focus soar.

Say No

Life is about saying yes. I'd like to add that it's also about *knowing when to say no*. One thing you should do whenever people come to you with potential work, give yourself time to think. Learn to say, "No, I'm going to think about this first before I agree to this." If you are going to feed the next project with your time and resources, you need to make sure that what comes of it will give you a lot more than you're putting into it.

Don't be a "Yes-man." Be more discerning than that. Develop your criteria for getting involved in work. Develop the habit of thinking in terms of returns on investment. Your time, energy, money, and focus are investments. Ask yourself if you want to be a part of what you're being offered. It's better for you to spend each day on those things you love, the things that engage and empower you. Pay more attention to people and projects that = years down the line - you will look back and be glad that you did. Put your focus where it will serve you best.

Chapter Seven: Time Management Hacks You Need to Know

Time management is all about getting organized and mapping out your time for certain tasks. Time management matters a whole lot — unless you're like my buddy Josh, who just likes to wing it, and is somehow always in the right place at the right time. Now, we're not all like Josh. Some folks have simply got to get serious about how they spend their time if they are going to be productive at all! With time management, you don't work hard. You work smart. Now, if you're going to go on some boomer rant about how hard work is what pays off, then you need to have a seat. In today's world, the best rewards go to those who know how to work smart. They know how to achieve so much in so little time, even when they're staring down the double barrel of the shotgun called a deadline. You simply must learn to manage your time, if you want to be more effective, and if you want less stress in your life.

Same Time, Different Results

You may have wondered how it is that we all get the same number of hours in a day, yet some people are able to make a lot more happen for themselves than others. It all comes down to proper time management. If you're going to achieve your greatest goals, then like other high achievers, you must learn the skill of managing your time. You must master the art of working with time in a seamless dance, even when the pressure is really on.

When you decide to manage your time properly, the first thing you'll notice is a shift in mindset - from being busy to *getting results*. When you're always doing all kinds of things, your day will lack productivity, since your attention is not streamlined. You've got ham, eggs, baked beans, and blood sausages on your plate... and you also have ice cream, chewing gum, and... a sock? How do you expect to digest all of that? Time management allows you to direct your focus to the things that really matter so that you do more in less time.

The Benefits of Time Management

Why should you bother learning to manage your time?? Well, first, you will experience a phenomenal increase in your efficiency at work and your productivity as well. Next, when you develop a reputation for always managing your time properly, you will find that people respect you more for that, and they also respect your time. This way, you don't waste focus on doing needless things. You're a lot less stressed since you know what to do or what to expect at every point in time. You also have a lot more opportunities for you to advance in your career and in life in general. The doors magically pop up where they weren't before, and worlds of opportunity await you behind each one.

When you don't bother with time management, you will be anything but efficient. Your workflow becomes more like a work stutter, at best. You keep missing deadlines. You turn in shoddy work, and you develop a really horrible reputation, which reduces your chances of advancing in your career. To add the cherry on the cake, you have even more stress than others who manage their time. These alone should convince you that you need to learn how to manage our time better.

Managing your time means you can get a lot more done than anyone else. When you know what you need to do, you know how to handle your workload. This means you'll be able to do the right things on time and even have more time left over for other stuff too.

You won't have to redo the work you've already done, because you were in a hurry, or because you waited till the last minute and didn't have enough time to put in good work. You can create needless problems for yourself when you don't handle your time properly. If you don't plan, simply assuming that you're going to get "a round tuit," what happens when something requires your urgent attention *in addition to that task* you've been putting off? Therefore, you need to be a pro time manager. It's just easier. You have fewer problems to deal with, and more free time to do whatever you please.

Time Management and Productivity

These two go hand in hand. You can't' expect to be productive without learning how to manage your time. Even if you know someone successful who seems to always wing it, chances are they have a structure in their minds which they may not be conscious of. It's like a little notification that goes off, letting them know it's time to do this, that, or the other. Now, not everyone is that fortunate, which is why time management should be studied and practiced. Don't kid yourself that you have your own notification icon in your head. Why are you reading this book, then? Exactly.

The ability to manage time means that you will smash your goals every time. You will always be on track with your life's mission. Your focus will be even more enhanced because you are aware of what needs to be done, for how long, before you move on to the next thing. Since your brain is aware that you're only going to handle XYZ for 789 minutes or seconds, it's easy for it to persevere and keep going until you switch to the next task. The focus stays at an even level, and you're able to knock all your goals right out the part!

How to Become a Time Management Guru

It's not as hard as you think it is. All you need is to be willing to learn and put in a little work. After all, practice makes perfect. Now let's go over a few things you can do to become a pro at managing your time.

1. Plan. This much should be obvious. You need to plan if you're going to manage your time properly. You need to figure out what your plan is. Now, I'm not talking about creating a routine that leaves little room for improvisation. I'm talking about choosing to be smart about your decisions when it comes to knowing when you should do something so that you're working smart and not hard. There are countless apps for managing projects. Take advantage of these, so that you can plan smart and achieve results. When you take a minute to plan, you save 10 more in acting. This means your return on investment in terms of energy and focus will be 1,000 percent.

2. Make priorities. It's not enough to plan. You must sort out what's more important from what isn't. A lot of people do the stuff that has no importance or major impact on their lives first, and that just sucks their time, energy, and soul. You must understand what's important and what isn't. This way, you're spending energy doing things that need to be done.

3. Be a mono-tasker. You save a lot more time when you focus on doing one thing at a time, versus when you do several things at a time and end up feeling like you've gotten nowhere, even if you're feeling

more drained than an abandoned Toyota that's been parked by the side of some dirt road for years.

4. Make use of a time tracking app. These can help you make sure you remain on course and on target. Invest in them, maximizing every minute of your life.

5. Even break time must be scheduled. Don't make the mistake of only planning your work. Plan your break as well. It helps because you get to relax without feeling anxious or guilty about doing so. Also, your brain can stay more focused on the job at hand, because it knows that soon, you get to relax.

6. Consider when you're most productive. Don't just plan willy nilly. Plan so that you get your most important tasks out of the way during your peak performance hours. If you try to put the important stuff during a block of time during which you will be plainly exhausted, then you will find yourself not just burnt out, but unwilling or unable to continue with your goals.

7. Be comfortable with your limits. There will be times when you fail to make things happen within the specified time frame. That's alright. Learn from that and restructure your plans accordingly. Just don't make a habit of not hitting your targets. You need to make sure you set reasonable time frames for everything you need to accomplish each day, and you'll be alright. Don't beat yourself up, or you'll never master time management.

You Can Buy Everything but Time

That's just the way it goes. This is something Bill Gates and Warren Buffet will tell you — and they could buy damn near everything and anything that tickles their fancy. So how do you make the most of the time in general?

Begin by scripting your week. Consider that you only get about 52 of these per year. So, you'd better make them count by thinking long term. Handle the big stuff first, then move on to the smaller ones.

Start each day by being proactive, and then you can end with being reactive. Create 10-time blocks for each day, so that you can be a lot more productive.

Always invest your time. Is there something you've meant to read? You could steal time everywhere you can. You can listen to audiobooks whenever you're stuck in traffic, working out, or waiting in line for one thing or the other. The idea is to never have idle time.

Put in the work and the time. You need to put in 10,000 hours so that you can become a pro at whatever you're doing. It's that deep work state, where your focus is soon intense, that you get so much done in just a couple of hours than most people can accomplish in a couple of weeks.

Focus on wasting less time, not making more time. The way to do this is to always invest in your time. Seriously, work out how much time you might be wasting on, say, social media.

Let's say that only spend an hour a day on social media. Mind you, most people spend more than an hour, and perhaps you do as well. This is all hypothetical, so stick with me here. In seven days, you will have spent seven hours on Instagram. In a year, you will have spent 365 hours on Instagram. Now, if you were getting paid $80 an hour, or had a business that paid you that amount for each hour, in that year you have made $29,200. **Maybe it's time to start thinking of time as money.**

Plan your weeks like Bill Gates. Chunk your time. For instance, if you're a YouTuber, you can do several videos at once, as you're already in the state of flow. It's easier to do it now; you're all set up. Do you run a blog? Then you might as well keep writing, and then schedule your posts. Batch your tasks, and you'll be more productive.

Go paperless. You lose a lot of time when you're looking for this file and that document. That's a real-time stealer, and there's research to prove it. If your important documents are on actual paper, go digital. Take scans and photos, upload them onto multiple services like Google Drive, Box, and Dropbox, so you know you're protected.

Save yourself time and money that paper costs you; you're saving trees at the same time.

Use several monitors. The great Bill Gates has 3 monitors. One is for all the emails he gets, the other is for browsing, and the final one is for his tasks. It's great because you get to focus on that one thing and one thing alone.

Above all, get proactive. Learn to say no. Learn to take charge, and you'll have more success, wealth, and productivity in your life.

Chapter Eight: Hustle Culture — The Big Dos and Don'ts

It's a sad situation that millennials are often accused of being entitled and unwilling to work. Despite the insistence of some people that millennials are lazy, this is simply not the case. A lot of them work. A lot. Don't be so quick to assume that this is a good thing, though. Millennials work to the point where they get super burnt out. They are so dedicated to their work, forever in hustle mode. That's what I would like to talk about in this chapter. Hustle culture — which is basically a making workaholism a lifestyle.

Before you skip ahead to the next chapter, don't assume that it's only millennials that are part of the hustle culture and that none of this applies to you. It happens even to the best of us. With that said, I only mentioned millennials because it's funny, ironic, even, that the same set of people the world's 'boomers' see as lazy are some of the hardest working folk. I'm not glorifying hard work. I'm all for smart work. Don't get it twisted. The world we live in today allows entrepreneurship to flourish, especially with social media and the internet — both a huge part of the millennial's life.

What Hustle Culture Is

Hustle culture says it's perfectly okay for you to burn out. In fact, you could say it advocates you working your fingers to the bone until your back and butt become one with your office seat. When it comes to hustling culture, it means that your life is no longer in balance. You're all about the work and the Benjamins. Nothing else matters. For this reason, a lot of young people feel like they're running on empty, living meaningless lives, dying for something they can belong to besides the office.

To deal with hustle culture, you'll often find the millennial doing whatever they can to fill the gaping hole in their lives. They could become obsessed with fitness, social justice, travel, meditation, or whatever. They get to the point where they start to really wonder about their life path and who they really are. They seek the secret to happiness.

It's perfectly fine to have these obsessions, especially when they're balanced with every other aspect of your life. However, when your obsession is work, then you are in for a world of hurt. Sadly, hustle culture is about setting up a graven image to the god of work and bowing down until you can no longer stand up straight, no matter how much you want to. The idea behind hustle culture is that the only way to be respected by yourself, and others as well, is to be on the grind, 24/7. You're all about your business, and nothing more. According to hustle culture, that is the only way to succeed. It's the only way to be another Elon Musk. And it doesn't help that Elon Musk endorses this as well. What works for him is not necessarily the rule. But in the world of hustle, if you're not dominating at work, then you're not dominating in life.

A Battle against Stereotypes

It's quite possible that the reason the millennials work as hard as they do is because they're sick and tired of being put into boxes by the older generation. Since they're always being called lazy, in their minds, the fix is to be the extreme opposite; hence, the hustle culture. The problem is that in this culture, there is a lot of burnout, stress, depression, anxiety, and loneliness. A lot of young people suffer when it comes to relationships and friendships because their bosses and colleagues see them more often than their lovers, family, and friends do. So yes, they hustle, get the big bucks, the cool condo, but there's no one to share these things with. That's in the best-case scenario. Often, they hustle, and the juiciest fruits of their labor go to their bosses at the top, not them.

The Good Thing about Hustle Culture

Now, hustle culture is not entirely bad. In fact, it can work wonders when you adopt the mindset. The secret here is knowing how to balance work with everything else. I would suggest chunking up the hustle. When you're at work, you're at work. You're dealing with your set tasks for the day. However, when the day is over, you're done being a part of the hustle culture. This is the only way you can become a part of that scene without having your heart and soul completely crushed by the ever-grinding gears of the corporate world.

How Social Media Fuels Extreme Hustle Culture

Workaholism is the latest, fanciest cult in town. It's fueled in large part by social media. Hop on Instagram, and you'll immediately be inundated by pictures of people hustling in one way or another. A picture of a laptop, a cup of coffee, some pencils, and a sketchpad. Hashtag hustle. You get the idea. Stay on social media long enough, and you start to get the feeling that you're worth nothing, because you haven't been doing any good, or you're not doing as much as you should. You look at all the posts, and you start to want some of that action for yourself. Just when you log off and go to lick your wounds or find ways to work harder, there's Google sending you a push notification with news about how some Forex trader just made $1,000,000,000,000 in a couple of days, and you're thinking, "Now hold on a minute, that's an impossible number of zeroes!" Then you think about how much of a zero you are. Now, you're off to hustle, with a depressed, defeated state of mind.

Don't Buy into the Hype

You'll notice that when it comes to people who post this kind of flashy stuff about their work and achievements, you never see anything about them getting rejected, or any talk about them being out of a job, or the fact that they may be miserable even while raking in the dollars. That's because no one wants to see that when they log on to social media to escape their problems.

The longer you remain on social media, the more it begins to shape your idea of what success should be like. Unfortunately, the picture you're being shown tells you that true success is all hustle, hustle, hustle, and no breaks. Please, do not misunderstand me: there is absolutely nothing wrong with wanting to celebrate your achievements, or post about how fired up you are today after your meeting with the one and only Buffet, but the troubling thing here is the way in which these posts are created.

Yes, you should go after your dreams. Pursue them! Make them happen! However, be smart about it. Don't work till your health starts to suffer for it. Don't work until you're depressed and anxious all the time. Don't do something that has you celebrating the start of a new work week, versus celebrating that it's something you enjoy doing. That's the problem with social media. It makes the hustle culture of working with no breaks seem like a religion all must belong to, or risk being labeled a heretic. It's like we live in that episode of Black Mirror, where we're all being rated by what we post online. It's disturbing, but it's the reality of today's world. What most people in this culture don't realize is how badly they are getting ripped off by the wealthy, since they're all about working to the point of exhaustion.

Are you an enthusiast of the hustle culture? Be honest with yourself. You may need to make some changes so that you don't risk burning out completely. You see, being always all about work at all hours does absolutely nothing for your creativity or your productivity.

Balance is key. If you can balance your work life and other aspects of your life, then you've found the sweet spot. Contrary to what social media and hustle culture would have you believe, you can achieve success without burning out. If you've been paying attention throughout this book, then you - no doubt - know that by now.

Workaholism and Toxic Productivity

You know the American dream, right? Work hard, do your best, and you will become successful and super-wealthy. Unfortunately, that narrative is not realistic for a lot of people. Never mind that most people buy into a meritocracy, believing that the best rewards always go to the people who are the most talented and work the hardest. The truth of the matter is that it is just not the way it works. Not in real life! For this reason, everyone has a burning desire to prove that they are worthy. They want to prove that they have the skills and the abilities, and so they should get the success that is due to them by pure merit. It's funny how despite the evidence against meritocracy that is real life — with people in positions they are beyond unqualified for — you probably still think that when you work hard, you're going to get what's yours: The top. Success. Wealth.

This is a sample inspirational quote you may or may not have seen on social media:

Get up earlier.

Stay longer.

Work harder.

Fail.

Fail again.

Never ever quit.

Well, look at that! I bet you want to print this out and put it up on your vision board, huh. Look, I even made it bold and italicized it for you. Go ahead! Print it! Then trash it. Because this is the way, the grind will grind you up and spit you out. This is not the way to be productive! This is not the way to go after your goals! Print this and stick it on your coffee maker instead:

The Grind Will Grind You

Get it? On your coffee machine? Because of coffee grinds? Never mind. I'm clearly not focused on my comedy hustle.

Have your dreams. Work towards them. That's a great thing! The problem is the obsession with constant productivity and work is bad for you. It adds this pressure to the need to work overtime or keep up with others. Next thing you know, you're working night and day. It's way too demanding that you can't last. It's so bad that you can't just be at home with family and friends. You might even work a side gig or have projects of your own that you need to work on, which means you're working nights as well.

Work/Life Balance

A lot of people across the world find themselves in a situation where they live to work, instead of work to live. It's not always a matter of choice in this situation. There's barely any time to really enjoy your life when you've spent your whole week at a job you hate. There are those who work hard deliberately because they want to enjoy themselves after the next 3 decades. Or they may have to provide for their family. It's just funny that despite how much money you make, you don't have enough time to even enjoy the fruits of your labor.

The culture we live in makes it hard to establish balance in life. It's sad that a lot of inspirational videos keep barking, "Work harder! Work longer!" when there are doing 70 plus hours a week and doing harder work than the poster boys and girls of success.

Healthy Hustle

Now let's talk about the healthy hustle. You know, the kind where you're not beating yourself into a pulp, day after day. Hustle is about focus and drive. It's about committing to yourself, and to the goals you've set out for yourself, each new day. You make that commitment anew, each day, whether things are on track or slightly delayed. Hustle is about giving your all emotionally and mentally, even when you're tempted to do something easier. The good kind of hustle is what sets you apart from the hobbyist. You understand that there's no such thing as perfection and that it's a journey. You only take pit stops as needed. You know when it's time to take a break and recharge, and when it's time to floor it.

Why You Should Hustle the Right Way

A healthy hustle is what sets you apart from the world of average. It puts you a cut above the rest when it comes to your profession. Let's assume you're a writer. Why should you be chosen, over someone else, when you're comfortable with your skills and don't bother trying to improve or sharpen them? Why should you be chosen over someone else with equal skills as you? Let's say you're on Upwork or something. When you're just like every other writer out there, you find that it all comes down to luck.

Let's say you've been hustling, though. You've been working hard to improve yourself. You've been reading, bettering yourself, working on getting better in your niche. You've done the work, and it's obvious. You know what you're talking about, and in a single conversation, it's evident to your client that you're not like all the other writers they've been chatting with. You're going to get the gig. It's a no brainer. Every client wants the best!

You must maintain the spirit of hustle. By this, I mean that you need to discipline yourself, so that on days when something happens to knock you off your game, it's easier for you to bounce right back and get to it. This hustle is what will propel you to the top of your career. This is what will get you over mountains and across seas.

Hustle Culture Do's

Do have a vision: First, you must have a vision. A goal that is yours. A goal that calls to you. It's all you can think about, night and day. It makes you eager to roll out of bed in the morning. It gives you so much joy and pride to work towards it. Some people will think your goal is crazy. That's okay. You alone know what the goal means to you. It's not for other people to understand. It's for you to fall deeper in love with and passionately pursue.

Your vision has got to be bold. The reason you want a bold one is that, as I said before, the goal is for you to become a better person. The goal of the goal is growth. You need something that will leave you changed for the better. The goal might seem scary at first, but with the right attitude and the right system, you will find yourself making steady progress.

Do focus: We've already gone over this. No focus, no progress. Focus is the only shot you've got at making your dreams come true. Pay attention to your goals to the exclusion of everything else around you when you're at work. Give it your all.

Do be indifferent and determined: Not towards yourself or the things you aspire to achieve. You need to be indifferent to the critics around you. There will be critics. Some of them will even be friends and family. Some of them don't even know when they're playing the critic. That doesn't matter though, because you're indifferent to it. If you've always cared what people think about your choices, then when it comes to your goals, learn not to listen. Stop your ears and focus on the journey. You must be your own cheerleader before you get anyone rooting for you. So, grow a backbone, be determined to make progress, if only a little bit, every day - *every chance you get.*

Do take complete responsibility. You have to own your actions. Own the consequences of what you do, good, bad, or neutral. If you notice what you're doing is not working, that's not the time to blame the economy, blame a colleague, or blame whoever's sitting at the White House. That's the time to find a new, better way to achieve the same goal. Own everything that is yours, and you will find that obstacles don't bother you. You find a way to get around them, over them, under them, or just bulldoze right through them.

Do have grit. Every true hustler has grit. Even when they seem to have failed, they get back up and at it every time. Having grit means you understand there are times your goal will seem tough. There are times when it will feel like you took several steps backward. When you've got grit, you learn to get back up on the saddle and giddy-up. That's how you move forward.

Hustle Culture Don'ts

Don't deprive yourself of sleep. Sleep matters. Sleep is how your mind gets refreshed so that you can have even better ideas on how to move forward, and the drive to do just that. Hustle is about what you do when you're awake. It's not about trying to create more time by losing sleep. Sleep is important if you want to give the very best of you to your goals.

Don't separate your ambition from your happiness. When you hustle, you make sure that your ambition and your happiness are a match. A lot of people talk about hustle, but they don't actually hustle. Why? Because they're not happy about what they're doing, so they don't' give their all. If you really love what you do, here's a little secret: It won't even feel like work. You give your all; you maximize your actions and your tie to make sure you're making your dreams happen. You're all about making every second count. You've got to be all in, without sacrificing your happiness. If you're happy working 100 hours a week, do that. If you'd rather make it 40, do that. I know a guy who works 3 hours a week. He created systems that allowed him to do that. Figure out who you are and what works for you. Then do that.

Don't sacrifice the things and people that matter. Your health matters. Your relationships matter. Your friends and family matter. Don't sacrifice all these people on the altar of hustle. There's no guarantee that you'll think it was worth it at the end when you're all alone, sick, and miserable.

Don't expect success to be overnight. Remember, it's a process. The goal is to make progress. It won't happen overnight. (A lot of the overnight successes you read about had actually been putting in a lot of work *before* they became successful!) Don't pressure yourself. Be real about your targets and expectations, and you are bound to succeed eventually.

Chapter Nine: 10 Steps to Self-Discipline

A huge part of being productive involves self-discipline. Self-discipline is all about being able to see things through, regardless of distractions, or the thousands of reasons your mind tells you to do something else. It's about being able to restrain yourself, so you don't oversleep, or overeat, or overindulge in hours of laziness. It's about giving things some thought before you take any action. Self-discipline means endurance, regardless of all the terribly inconvenient obstacles you will undoubtedly face along your journey. In a nutshell, self-discipline is about being able to control yourself, so that you don't give in to excesses that could wreck you or what you're trying to do.

Are You Self-Disciplined?

Think about this for a moment: Are you the sort of person who must have it now, every time? Can you release the need for instant gratification so that you can reap more rewards later on? Would you be willing to forgo immediate pleasure, and put in more time and effort, so you can get better outcomes later? If you can, then you're self-disciplined.

When people think about self-discipline, they sort of cringe on the inside. It's like those two words mean you can't live at all. You might even assume that self-discipline means you never get to enjoy life and that you could never be a self-disciplined person because who the heck wants to work so hard and continually sacrifice the very things that make life worth living, right? The truth is that you can develop self-discipline, and the process does not actually require hard, back-breaking, soul-draining work. In fact, it could even be fun. I know, shocker, right?

True Self Discipline

Actual self-discipline is not about never having fun or serving out a lifelong sentence of restriction. It's not about keeping your point of view so narrow that anything else outside of it does not exist for you. What true self-discipline is, is the demonstration of resilience and inner strength, as you handle your daily tasks, getting closer and closer to achieving your goal.

The Cure for Laziness and Procrastination

If you're a very lazy person, then a shot of self-discipline with a generous splash of willpower should help pull you out of that negative state of mind. You'll learn how to stick with things until you get results. You will learn mental toughness and grit, which will carry you through even the biggest and toughest of obstacles.

Procrastination becomes a non-issue when you're self-disciplined because you are always on the move. You find it easier and easier to take decisive action, rather than just sit around running your hand through your hair in frustration. You learn the very necessary virtue of moderation. You become a lot more understanding and more considerate of others. You grow in patience, which is still a fashionable virtue these days.

A Self-Disciplined Turtle

When you're self-disciplined, one of the most notable things about you is that you're never late, and you never waste a minute of your time. You're always investing your time into things that will benefit you in the long run. You are in complete control of where your life goes, *and it goes exactly where you want it to.* You don't just set goals and sit back, expecting them to magically happen. You act.

Consistency matters a lot more than speed. This is the lesson that we learned in the story of the rabbit and the turtle in a race. The rabbit figured the turtle was way too slow, and he would beat it. While the rabbit decides to take a nap in the middle of the race, the turtle just kept going. The turtle made it to the finish line. Somewhere on the internet is an actual rabbit-versus-turtle race, where the turtle made it first. Look it up. It's fun stuff.

You're a turtle when you're self-disciplined, advancing confidently towards your goals, even if it's taking you longer than you or others say it should. You make a point of always finishing whatever you begin.

Why People Aren't Self-Disciplined

This is how to begin the habit of self-discipline. I know it seems too easy, but that's just the way it is. A lot of people have so many excuses for why they have not yet started or finished this, that, or the other. They'd rather wing it. That's not going to work if you actually want to get stuff done.

Another reason people find it hard to exercise self-discipline is that they have way too much to do. If your calendar is like a burger with 5 stacks of beef in between a couple of buns, then there's no way you're going to wrap your mouth around it. Again, busy is not cool. Don't pile on the work until you can barely stand up straight. This is the reason a lot of people cannot be self-disciplined since they've already set themselves up for failure.

The folks who are neither self-disciplined nor productive tend to have a bajillion tasks on their to-do list, and those tasks are not even prioritized. So if you're going to be a self-disciplined go-getter, then you need to take some time at the end of each day to sort out exactly what you need to do the next day.

Know Your Limits

If you know for a fact that you can only handle about 15 tasks a day, then focus on crossing those off your list. Don't try to be a superhero and do 100 things a day when you know for a fact that you might need a week before it's all done.

Self-Discipline and Productivity

There's this erroneous idea floating around in the atmosphere that productivity comes down to the kind of person that you are or the kind of work you do. It's all a matter of being disciplined! When you're disciplined, you remain focused on whatever it is you need to do for the day. It means you can sit down and work when it's time to do that.

Self-discipline is about more than what you can get done each day. It's also getting out of bed when you should in the morning, with not a moment of hesitation. It's making your bed. It's committing to your workout program. It's saying no to an extra cookie. It's the way that your life gets better. It's the way forward. If you notice that you could use some more productivity in your work life, then decide to become a self-disciplined person. Work on it, if you ever want to be productive.

How to Be Self-Disciplined

Make your bed, every morning, or whenever it is, you wake up. Again, not everyone is a morning person. Before you set foot out the door, make up or review a list of two to three things you would like to achieve by the end of the day, then make sure that each day, you get those things done. This is just one little way to build your self-discipline.

It's like a muscle. You've got to train it. When you train, you don't go straight to deadlifting 500 pounds, or you're going to break your back, and no gym in the world will be blessed by your presence or your dollars ever again. You start with what you're comfortable with. Then, if you're going to get bigger and stronger, you progressively increase the weights you lift. The more you lift, the stronger you get. This is the same thing with self-discipline. In fact, I recommend starting a workout regimen, as well. Watch as that alone affects other aspects of your life.

The more you do the little things to build your self-discipline, the more you will experience the benefits in other aspects of your life. So start by making your bed, and doing your two or three daily tasks. You might find yourself spontaneously deciding to work out and make a habit of it. You might find you're willing to read at least 2 books a month now.

If at any point, you refuse to do the things you know you should, you will grow weaker in self-discipline. It's still like a muscle in that regard. Use it less, and you lose strength and size. So do your best not to make a habit of ignoring what you need to do. It may seem nice to not do the needful for once, but the pleasure you get from skipping tasks is not worth the pain you feel from having to start back at zero. So don't give in to the temptation to quit. Keep going.

What to Expect As You Discipline Yourself

In the beginning, it will be uncomfortable. See, self-discipline is not the same thing as motivation. You could easily get motivated to do something, start something. However, whether you have the self-discipline to see it through is another matter altogether. There's none of the trademark enthusiasm with motivation when it comes to disciplining yourself. You might feel nothing at best, or like you'd rather be biting your nails, at worst. Yet, you've got to keep going. Push through the discomfort.

In the beginning, you will feel all sorts of emotions about being self-disciplined. You might decide you hate the way you feel, and that you just want it all to end. The good news, though, is that once you've repeated your daily tasks enough times that they become a habit, you stop feeling all of that. You act on autopilot. It becomes a natural thing for you to be disciplined. That's the goal.

You're going to fail. Be prepared for that. Some days, you will just not be able to keep up. There's nothing wrong with that. The problem is when you decide since you have failed for 10 days in a row, you're going to give up. Don't give up. And don't start over, either. Simply pick up from right where you left off. Stop trying to gun for a 100 percent winning streak of days where you never slip up. You're going to slip up. Just get back on your feet each time and keep going. It starts off uncomfortable, but the great news is that over time, it actually gets easier.

Doing What You Love versus Loving the Process

When you do what you love, you will never work a day in your life. It's the truth. Don't credit me. Marc Anthony said that. With that said, there will be some things that you will not love, which are just as vital as the things you do love. So what do you do about that? Choose not to do them? No! You have to fall in love with the journey. The process is what makes it easy to handle.

Now, I love writing. I love the feeling of knowing I've banged out my allotted number of pages for the day. It feels good. With that said, in my early writing days, I never particularly enjoyed the process of editing. Every good writer will tell you that writing happens in two stages: Writing, and then editing. So how did I get around that? Simple. I would just recall the feeling of what it's like when I'm done. I love that feeling. So I discipline myself to make sure I get the work done. Now, I don't even have to think about it. I just "get it done." There is nothing like the feeling of accomplishment and seeing how far my writing has come. I'm in love with the process. How can you apply this?

- Appreciate your craft.
- Be proactive about improving your skills to the point of mastery.
- Work to earn creativity, autonomy, impact, and recognition for your work.

Steps to Develop Self-Discipline

To develop self-discipline, recognize that there are two basic ways in which you can go about accomplishing your daily tasks.

- You could tell yourself, "Oh, I'll do it when I feel like it."
- Or, you could say, "I will do it, and as I do it, I'll start to feel like it."

One of these ways will get you further in life than you could ever possibly imagine. Not that I need to point it out, but the second way is the way to go. With that said, how can you really develop self-discipline?

1. Begin small. We've all got some really big goals we want to smash. You probably want to climb Mount Everest, write 10 books in a year, read 5 in a month, and have 5 tech startups at Elon Musk's and Jeff Bezos' level of success by lunchtime. Right? Well, obviously, you don't, but you get my point.

The key to self-discipline is to start small and work your way up. Want to lose weight? Don't start by wanting to lose a pound a week. The only way I know that can happen is by water fasting or dry fasting. I'm not a doctor, so please, don't try any of that without seeking professional medical advice.

A good rule of thumb when it comes to building self-discipline is to halve the goal and double the time you think it will take you. You think your goal is to lose a pound a week? Then make it half a pound in two weeks. Why? You're more likely to achieve your goal, and you're less likely to give up on being self-disciplined and quit before you see results.

Even when it comes to weight loss, don't jump right into doing Shaun T's Insanity or something. You could simply decide to cut out soda and replace it with water. When you master that, you can move on to eliminating unhealthy treats. When you've done that, then you can work in three cups of green tea. The point is, start small, and progress will definitely happen. As you conquer the little steps and celebrating the little things, you will build the confidence to continue with self-discipline.

2. Practice every day. When you practice every day, you're building a new habit that will serve you in the long run. Remember the rabbit and the turtle? It's not about speed. What matters is consistency. Every day do what you need to do even if it seems like a lot less than what you would prefer to do. Don't give yourself excuses.

Force yourself to go. If you don't have the energy to work out, then still go. It's better to do a workout tired than to not do it at all.

3. Slowly ramp things up. Once you're good with the small stuff and are more confident in your ability to stay disciplined, then you can take things up a notch. The key is to continue challenging yourself.

Say you decided you were going to start working out. So you start off taking a brisk 15-minute walk every day. Now, that has become your habit. It's time to kick things up a notch by adding some more time! When you get used to that, you can escalate to jogging, then running, then doing HIIT exercises... And maybe then you can bust out the Insanity workout DVD. Again, I'm not a doctor, and I'm not a trainer, so get professional advice. This may not necessarily work for you.

4. Get rid of temptations. Keep junk food out of the house, and you can't eat junk. Keep your cell phone out of sight, and you won't be distracted by all those notifications as you work. Do your best to get rid of the things that make you lose focus and discipline. When you mess up and give in, get right back on the horse.

5. Make a plan. You already know this. You need a solid plan of action. A plan helps you stay on course, and can clearly make you see when you're not being disciplined about your time or the projects you have set out to do. Whether it's weight loss, quitting cigarettes, building your business, or working on a relationship, you must have a plan that outlines the steps you need to take in order to achieve your goals.

6. Respect your weaknesses. There will be things that strike your Achilles' heel with the precision of a homing device. Don't try to deny them. Recognize them and own them. This way, you can factor them into your plans, and keep said plans practical. If you don't acknowledge and plan for your weaknesses, then you're going to be incredibly frustrated with yourself. Know what can get you to lose focus. Know what you can and can't achieve. Plan accordingly, and have a headache-free life.

7. Ditch bad habits for good ones. Rather than simply focusing on quitting your bad habits, a more effective solution would be to replace them with good ones. It's like taking stuff out of a hole that needs to feel whole. You don't want to take out the bad and have some other bad habit sneak in. So figure out the best replacements for you. Maybe instead of switching from smoking cigarettes to marijuana, you could switch to chewing gum. Or you could switch from ice cream to yogurt. You'd be much better off making substitutes, than leaving that hole unfilled.

8. Let your future self thank you. When it comes to willpower, it's cyclical. You only have so much to give at each point before you need to recharge. So how do you fix this? Set yourself up for success! Do things that will make your future self say, "Hey, thanks for being so thoughtful!" In other words, set things up so that it's easy for you to do what you intend to do. Want to work out in the morning? Fall asleep in your clean gym clothes, or put them right under your pillow so you can get dressed. Need extra help getting out of bed? Keep your caffeine pills close if you need them. Want to get to writing immediately when you sit down to work? Then set up your computer so that the first thing you see when you log in is the book you're working on.

9. Set up the right systems. When it comes to why we do the things we do, we are actually anything but rational. It all comes down to impulse and emotions. You, like everyone else, are naturally in pursuit of pleasure and rewards. So, if you want to achieve something for the day, go ahead and set up a reward system. Treat yourself to something nice every time you show self-discipline and do what you intend to do. Obviously, something nice can't be a sweet treat or even food, if you're trying to lose some weight.

10. If you want to discourage yourself from being undisciplined, then set up a system that would discourage you from doing so. There are actually apps that can charge you money for missing out on a workout or your goals! That's definitely a great investment. Perhaps better than having a friend keep you accountable. After all, you can't

talk an app out of taking the money from you. If that doesn't keep you in line, then you probably have way too much money to burn for that strategy to be effective. Find something that works for you.

Chapter Ten: How to Cultivate Mental Toughness

Let's talk about mental toughness. It's the ability for your brain to pick up a ten-pound barbell and pump it endlessly. No, I'm kidding. Mental toughness is all about being able to deal with our concerns, doubts, worries, and circumstances successfully. It's about perseverance, through doubt, and hardship. This is how you achieve excellence in your field of endeavor.

For the longest time, no one thought of mental toughness outside of sports psychology. In that field, mental toughness is thought of as a natural ability, or a psychological edge that you develop, which lets you deal with obstacles much better than your challengers, especially when it comes to training, competition, and the lifestyle of a sports person. It's about being better than the next guy or gal, and being more determined, confident, consistent, focused, and totally in charge even when the pressure is intense.

Mental Toughness Isn't Just for Sport

Mental toughness is something that can be of benefit to you in whatever aspect of life you apply it to. It's what gets leaders to the top. It's what keeps them there. Whether it's in the music industry, or the movie industry, business, or whatever really, you need some mind mettle in order to not just survive, but thrive.

What Mental Toughness is All About

A winning mindset. You need to set about your day like you know you've already won. You know you're going to perform at maximum capacity. You believe in your abilities, and you know whatever is required of you, you're going to do it, and ace it. Every. Single. Time.

The skill of stress optimization. Stress happens and is unavoidable. As a mentally tough person, you know how to deal with stress. You can handle the pressure as you do what needs to be done, without feeling paralyzed by fear or choked by anxiety. Or you might feel both emotions intensely, but you know how to bulldoze past them and get the job done and done beautifully, anyway. In fact, you masterfully turn the stress and pressure into fuel that powers you to deliver your very best on whatever goal it is you have in sight.

Excellent failure. Yes, winners fail, too. The difference between winners and losers is that the winners take a step back and analyze their results and process to see what worked and what didn't. Then they learn from it. They understand that a few failures here and there do not make them failures. There is a difference between being a failure and failing to perform. The winner with mental toughness is no whiny cry baby. They excel at failing. They get back up, and they do even better on account of having failed.

Giving it everything. When you're mentally tough, you give it all you've got. You know how to ignore the discomfort. You understand that it's only a temporary thing. You know that your goal will lift you to great heights, and because you understand that, you are mentally prepared for the hardship along the way, and ready to give it all, with no holds barred.

Always being prepared. Before you step into battle, you arm yourself to the teeth. You know that you've got to plan. This is not the time to wing it like a chicken wing. This is not the time to let the chips fall where they may. You have a plan, and you have a backup plan for your plan... And another for your back up plan. You are prepared for every eventuality, and this gives you the nerves of steel that let you remain in control under pressure. You have a plan for your failure. You also have a plan for your success.

The Benefits of Acquiring Mental Toughness

When you're mentally tough, you always deliver more. You commit. You're not just another lackey showing up, punching in, watching the time pass, so that they can punch out. You have a purpose as you work. You want to be the best, always, or at least as often as you can be. As a result, you always deliver on time, and you deliver quality as well.

Mental toughness means your wellbeing is optimum. You can deal with stress much better than average people. You're not the kind who is going to let challenges keep you from getting a good night's sleep. You're less likely to get stressed out, and you're the last person anyone wants to bully.

As a mentally tough person, you're generally more positive and engaged. You can't help but look for the good in everything so that you can move everyone on to the next level of greatness. Your positivity is contagious. You are more than happy to volunteer your services when you have the time and mental capacity to commit. You're always scouting for new opportunities that will serve you, and everyone.

You're an eager learner, as a mentally tough person. You're not content with the status quo. You love to learn, and as such, you do better every day, applying what you've learned to make yourself more productive.

You handle change better than most. Change is inevitable. Yet, there are those who would rather stick their heads in the sand and pretend that everything is fine exactly as is and that nothing needs to change. However, you know that's not the case. You have perfect, healthy coping mechanisms to deal with change as it happens, and are less likely to stress out in response.

You have high aspirations. Mentally tough people are naturally ambitious. They exude certain confidence in the pursuit of their goals. Because of your lofty aspirations and your drive, you remain committed to your goal, no matter what comes your way.

Mental Toughness and Productivity

It's important to develop the trait of mental toughness if you want to be productive. When you're mentally tough, you know how to channel your attention and your effort towards achieving your goal. You generally know how to inspire and motivate others to bring their best as well, and this improves productivity overall, wherever you are.

One very important factor in being able to stay productive is your attitude to failure. If you wuss out each time things do not go your way, then needless to say, you're not going to make it really far with your goals, or in life in general. However, with mental toughness, you know that resilience is key when dealing with failure. You know that failure provides the opportunity for different, better ideas than what you had and that when you seize this opportunity, only one outcome is certain: Success.

Productivity involves knowing when to brainstorm solutions to a problem, and also knowing when to let mistakes go. You can't keep dwelling on problems, because you'll never move forward that way.

Mentally tough people know that, and so they're willing to move past mistakes without a moment's hesitation so that they can get on with the business of making their goal happen, or reaching their target.

Negative emotions are the enemy of productivity. You need to be mentally tough in order to make sure these speed bumps don't turn into mountains in your path. Mentally tough people know that there is no use in feeding discord and discontent. They're the ones moving the meeting forward, past petty arguments that can hold people back. They're emotionally intelligent, which means there is no feeling strong enough to make them quit doing what needs to be done.

Finally, the ability to say no is key when it comes to increasing your productivity. This way, meaningless distractions, and needless commitments do not stop you from attaining your goal. The mentally tough know how to say no, and are comfortable doing so. They understand that it matters to have just what is needed on their plate, and nothing more. This way, they always finish whatever it is they start, remaining productive no matter what.

How to Build Your Mental Toughness

1. Maintain perspective. When you keep your issues in the right perspective, you will find that they are not big enough to get in the way of you doing what you need to do each day. Even when no one and nothing is on your side, push through regardless.

2. Learn to master your emotions. If you're going to be productive, then you must learn not to let your emotions get the better of you. Feel them, but don't act on them. This way, you can remain objective and make the right decisions each time.

3. Detach. Practice not making things about you. Understand that taking things personally is a time waster and an energy stealer. Pay attention to what you can control instead.

4. Be open to change. Things change. Get over it. You must become flexible in your thinking. You must be willing and eager to

adapt at all times, and then none of that change could ever get in your way.

5. Be ready for challenges. Life is not a smooth ride. Whether it's in business or in your personal life, there will be challenging issues. Your attitude is what will determine how you get through them. So prepare for challenges, and you will find yourself developing an unbreakable, can-do spirit.

6. Work on resilience. The next time you feel like you want to throw in the towel because you're letting challenge stress you out, pause. Step back for five minutes. Take a deep breath, relax, and then get back at it. Learn to deal with pressure properly, and you will demonstrate strength every time, even when others are stressed.

7. Be positive about setbacks and failures. It's all part of the journey. They're unavoidable. So how are you going to deal with them? Be proactive about reducing the damage of your mistakes, learn what you need to learn from the experience, and then get back to business.

8. You need to focus on. Keep your eyes on the ball. Think long term, and you'll still be in the race, even when others have quit.

9. Be patient. You cannot expect to get instant results with everything you do. You need to let things come to fruition in their own time. Don't try to rush things, because you will fail colossally. You can throw a hissy fit at the grass in your yard, yelling at it to grow... But it will grow at its own pace. So be patient.

10. Validate yourself. Forget about trying to make others happy. Don't be a waffle. Do your best to always stand by your own opinions and decisions.

11. Exercise control. This is all about self-discipline. You must learn that you're in charge of you. Do not give others your power. You alone are responsible for your words and actions or lack thereof. Learn to own your reactions.

12. Persevere through failure. You must see that every time you fail, you've been given a golden ticket to get better. You can't just quit.

You've got to take advantage of that ticket and keep going. With perseverance, you will definitely get it right.

13. Learn acceptance. You must be okay with the things you cannot control. You can only control one thing: Your reaction. That's it. So learn to control it so that it serves you every time. Accept the things that cannot change, so you can come up with great ways to work with or around them.

14. Never give up your positive spirit. Stay upbeat even when you meet people who are hell-bent on being so negative that they suck the life out of you. Lift them up to your level. Never stoop to theirs. Most importantly, do not allow their words or actions to be a factor in what you're trying to achieve for yourself.

15. Be tenacious. You must not quit. Ever. Can you take breaks? Sure. Can you quit? No.

16. Be content. Envy will not serve you. Stop wishing you had what others have, and focus on your own achievements and the goal you've set for yourself.

17. Trust your inner compass. Stay true to who you are. Stay true to your values. Trust your gut all the time. It will save you when you feel lost.

18. Never compromise your standards. There will be tough times. That's no excuse to set the bar lower for yourself. Keep it high. Raise it, even.

If you're going to be mentally tough, then you're going to need to practice. You need to become more mindful of the habits you have so that you can see which ones do not serve you and replace them with better habits.

Chapter Eleven: The Road to Success — 25 Strategies for Growth

What Success Is

Success is relative. It means whatever you assume it means. For the musician, it could be churning out hit singles and albums consistently. For the trader, it could be making enough from their trading to afford their desired lifestyle. For some people, it's about being able to travel wherever, whenever. For others, it's about being rich. For others still, it's about raising kids to be proud of. In other words, success is really about being personally fulfilled. It's about being able to live your best life, day after day.

A Success Mindset

You must have heard the term "success mindset" thrown around in the motivational speaking world, but what is it about, really, and why does it matter? With a success mindset, you're always very adaptable. You are flexible enough to see the opportunities that everyone else inexplicably misses. It doesn't matter what your field is; having a success mindset is how you get to the top. Sure, you may have had a hard knock life; however, with a success mindset, you can rise, regardless of your past. You can make it, regardless of the odds against you.

Three Keys to the Success Mindset

There are three parts to this mindset.
- The desire for growth.
- The ability to be self-reflective.
- An eye for possibilities.

The success mindset is the growth mindset. You cannot expect success if you're not open to growing. With a growth mindset, you know that you have the chance to get better with practice, over time. You don't waste that chance. However, if your mindset is a fixed one, then you believe your skills are at a set point. You don't believe you could get smarter, better, and more productive. You're stuck.

Another part of the success mindset is the ability to look within and reflect on yourself. You need to be aware of who you are, the habits you have that are holding you back, and those that are driving you forwards. You need to make sure that you continue to take responsibility for your actions and experiences, god, bad, or neutral. Figure out how you could have chosen a different tack that would have helped you get better. Ask yourself questions like, "What did I learn from this? Am I growing? How? What could I have tried instead?" Be completely honest with yourself. As you ask these questions, you will always be on the move forward and upward.

Finally, you must have a keen eye for the possibilities around you. You need to be aware of all the good possibilities you've got. It's not about being blindly optimistic. It's not about assuming that you can do everything, including fly like Superman. What it does mean is you should notice the different ways in which you can get better at your craft, day by day, and then take advantage of the chance to do better.

To develop a success mindset, you have to practice. There's no other way. Defeatist thoughts and attitudes simply need to be tossed aside. You need to see yourself as a winner — the kind who always thinks win-win in every scenario. Believe that you really can be better. Believe that success is yours, as long as you put in the work.

How to Develop a Success Mindset

You can't just sit down, take a few deep breaths and chant, "I have a success mindset" over and over again. You have to work on it. Here's how:

1. Take a little step each day that advances you towards your goals.
2. Put systems in place that will help you remain on track.
3. Get all the info you need that could help you move forward.
4. Make sure your to-do list is set up in order of importance.
5. It's best to write tomorrow's to-do list tonight.
6. Handle the big stuff first, and then take care of the little stuff after.
7. Choose to make better decisions by using mental filters.
8. Get in the habit of making decisions about your life. You're the director of your own life. So decide as though you're going to get a paycheck for doing that, just like a CEO would.
9. Always keep the worst possible scenario in mind before you take action.

10. When you're making decisions, learn to think conditionally. "If this I do this, then that will happen."

11. Always keep the finish line in mind, making sure that everything you do propels you towards it.

12. Be open to the gifts that your failures give you. They are learning opportunities.

13. Take a step back from your intense emotions, so that you can take action from an objective state of mind.

14. Do not indulge in negative self-talk. It's useless and defeatist.

15. Get feedback from people that you know are capable and trustworthy.

16. Understand yourself. Know your strengths and your weaknesses.

17. Be comfortable with correcting yourself when you find out that you're way off the mark.

18. Learn to be constructive in the way you deal with positive and negative criticism.

19. Learn skills that will help you achieve your target.

20. Focus on results.

21. Whenever you fail or experience a setback, please don't remain stuck on it. Just assess what you could have done differently and then move on.

22. It's okay to choose a different route when it's not just working out. Don't be afraid to correct your course.

23. Do keep in mind that you'd be better off maintaining your decision most of the time. If you do decide to change course, it will take you longer to see results. SO be sure about what you want to do.

Chapter Twelve: Forming Good Habits that Last

You want to be successful. It's the whole reason you've read this book to this point. I applaud you for that. I assume that in your quest for success, you now understand the importance of thinking about the long term. You get that you've got to be disciplined, for you to conquer milestone after milestone along your journey. The only way to move up the ladder of success is by constantly repeating the things that work, one rung at a time. In other words, to succeed, it all comes down to your habits.

If you want to start up a new business, or you want to make improvements to your health, then you must make sure you have the right habits. The question is, how can you not just replace bad habits with good ones, but also make them permanent? First, we're going to take a critical look at all the things people get wrong about habits.

Myths about Building Habits

"It takes 21 days for you to form a habit." How many times have you heard that one? Well, that's not the way it goes. There's no proper research backing that up. Before you argue, read the last sentence again and notice the word 'proper' is in bold letters.

Real research on how long it takes to form a habit suggests that there are a lot of variables that could affect how long it takes you to form a habit, from your environment to the habit, to your kind of person, among other things. I guess there's no way to spin that into a great book title, so a lot of people preach that 21 days hogwash.

You shouldn't be thinking of habits in light of how long it takes you to form them, anyway. If you do that, you'll notice that you're missing out on the point behind creating better habits to begin with: Creating lasting change in your life. It's a lifestyle thing, not a 21-day fad. You're not going to get results by crossing off each new day on your calendar. Now that I've sufficiently dashed your dreams of becoming a better person in three weeks, the question becomes, how exactly can you make sure your new habits actually stick?

Micro Targets, and Macro Goals

Let's talk about motivation for a minute. Research has found that if you want to be more disciplined, then you would be better off with abstract thinking. In other words, you can dream big. You can be all about the big picture, and forget about the minutiae.

With that said, a lot of people are uncomfortable with making plans they deem too grand, and as such, they get scared of the size of their dreams and their expectations, thinking there's more of a chance to fail than succeed. Sound familiar?

Lots of research shows that when you are motivated to make something happen by intrinsic elements, versus extrinsic elements like the anticipation of a reward or the fear of punishment, you will be able to stick with your goals and habits. You will find ways to walk the fine line between being a big dreamer, and doing the little things every day that get you closer to that big dream of yours. That means when you're intrinsically motivated to make your goals happen, you're cool with not having dramatic, overnight changes. You know that change for the better is inevitable. It's just going to come over a period of time.

With all of that said, in order to create habits that stick, you need to have micro targets, and macro goals. While the goals are the big picture, the targets are the little things you must do each day in order to make your goal happen.

Targets make it easy for you to stay on course each day. They help you actually achieve your goal. Here's the best thing about achieving your goal with targets: The best kinds of targets are the really low ones. You could commit to writing just 100 words a day if you're an aspiring author. You could write 101, or even go so far as to write 5000 in a day if you're feeling a bit fired up, but the point is you just need to write 100. As you do this, you're teaching yourself a new habit. Sure, you may only ever write 100 words a day every now and then, but for the most part, chances are you're hitting 5 or 10 times that target.

On Plans, Triggers, and Changes in Behavior

Habits and planning go hand in hand. Habits also have a lot to do with motivation. See, most people talk about a new habit they want to adopt but rarely do you ever hear them make any mention of why they want to make that new habit a thing.

I know it doesn't seem like much; however, this is what helps you remain motivated every day. The very last thing you want to do is to keep fantasizing about actually sticking with your new habit. You're less likely to stick with it if all you do is think about it. Also, don't just start in on a new habit without being clear about what you want to achieve. If you do, you will begin to lose your resolve, and you won't be consistent.

Recent research shows that while visualizing positively helps keep you motivated and inspired, it's not enough. It's a matter of what you visualize. You are far more likely to succeed if you also visualize the entire process of what you need to do to make your goal happen. For instance, if you want to lose five pounds, you don't just visualize yourself five pounds lighter. You visualize yourself working out, taking stairs instead of the elevator, saying no to junk food, eating healthy, and so on. This is the way to give your new habit the stickiness you need to achieve your goal.

Why does visualizing the process work? For one thing, visualizing helps you pay attention and keep your focus on the steps you need to take to make the goal happen. For another, when you visualize each of the steps you need to take, you find that you're less anxious about it, and are more likely to consider it a possible thing for you to stick with your new habit as part of your lifestyle.

Habits You Should Practice Daily to Stay Productive

You need to get habits in place so that when you run out of motivation, they will kick in automatically, and you'll still be on the right track. When you have the habits in place, it's easy to find motivation even if you're not feeling it... And you won't have to force it. Here are some habits to form that can keep you motivated and productive.

- Visualize. You have no idea just how powerful visualization is. Take time at the start of your day to visualize your goals and your future, and you will find yourself feeling inspired to push through with your target. All you need is three minutes a day, using the 3 phase visualization technique. In phase 1, consider what you'd like to be like for you, within the next 3 to 5 years. See what you've done, what you're doing, who you're with, and where you are. In phase 2, see the next 12 months and what they have in store for you. In phase 3, see what you have to get started on today so that you can make your dreams come true.

- Go over your goals. Do this each day, and last thing before bed. Go over why you're doing what you do and what you need to do to achieve them. Not only will you feel motivated, but you will also be able to stay focused, and have brilliant ideas on how you can get there.
- Take cold showers. If you're having trouble becoming fully awake, or if you're having trouble focusing, then take a cold shower. Once you do, you feel motivated and ready to perform. Make a habit of cold morning showers. It's not pleasant at first, but when you step out, you're more than ready to take charge of your day. Just remain calm, do some deep breathing, and detach your mind from how your skin feels. Give it 15 to 20 seconds, and it will become obvious the cold is not as bad as you dreaded.
- Read. Read something. Every day. I personally find I feel off if I don't get some reading in. When you read, your brain will have a lot of material to work with and give you fresh new ideas that can inspire you to greatness. Make it a habit to read in the morning and in the evening.
- Use affirmations. These are basically messages you repeat to yourself every day so that you remember what you're trying to achieve. You can leave yourself notes where you'll see them, keep your affirmations in your wallet, or as a reminder on your phone. Affirmations are basically messaged you find motivating and empowering. They can be popular quotes or your own mantra.
- Make your environment work for you. This will require some adaptability and flexibility on your part, especially when you're in a challenging environment. Your environment will always influence your productivity levels. So be mindful of the clutter on your desk, and the kind of people you allow into your space.

- Develop the habit of NOW. Got an idea? Go test it out now. Notice there's something you just have to do? Why not now? There's only ever now. You can tell yourself you'll do it later, but the truth is when later rolls around, it will still be now anyway! So why not do it this now so you can use the next now to do something else? That's how to remain productive.

Conclusion

Now, you have learned a lot of very useful strategies for you to not just set your goals, but make them happen. As you practice with these principles I've laid out in this book, you will find yourself accomplishing a lot more over the months to come than most people ever get done in a whole lifetime.

If you are going to succeed, you can't just read this. Read it again. More importantly, put it into practice. Take action, every chance you get. The more you take action, the quicker you can learn what works for you and what doesn't, so that you can succeed. People who accomplish things in life don't just sit around doing nothing, or just making little moves here and there. They are always on the go.

So get started on taking back your life. Your potential is limitless. There's always room for improvement. You don't have to make a quantum leap in a day. You only need a few steps each day to get you to your goal. You are the one who is responsible for what happens in your life. You can no longer claim to be ignorant of this fact. Blame your failures and setbacks on other people or the environment if you want, but deep down, you will always know that you and you alone are responsible. So act like you're in charge, and move confidently in the direction of your dreams.

Don't just apply these principles to your work life. Use them in every aspect of your life. Apply them to your finances. Go through your financial life with a fine-tooth comb, and then make up your mind how much it is you would like to be making within the next couple of years. Don't just let the chips fall where they may. Decide where they fall... If they even fall.

Work on your relationships, as well. Make it a priority to have productivity shine through not just when it comes to work, but in your relationship with your family, friends, and significant other. People matter. People are the reason you will move forward in life. So do invest in your relationships. Invest in expanding your network. You know that cliched but true saying: Your network equals your net worth. Also, there's no point finally achieving your dreams, only to end up sad and empty because there's no one with whom you can celebrate. What would be the point??

Your health is just as important. So make sure you decide and commit to a life that is healthy and full of energy. Make fitness a goal. Decide what fitness means to you, and work out a plan to make it happen. Remember, baby steps. We're not trying to build Rome in a day.

One thing I must mention before I completely wrap up this book is that you've got to use your subconscious mind to your advantage. Your subconscious mind is responsible for all the functions of your mind that you do not consciously handle. It's where innovative ideas come from. It's where the willpower comes from, too. You just have to mold it in such a way that it serves you. Your subconscious mind is amazing because it has unspeakable power. Power to bring you every single thing you've ever hoped for or dreamed of. So always enlist the help of your subconscious. How?

When you go to bed at night, see yourself through your own eyes, as having accomplished your goal. Fast forward. Go to the point in space and time that could only happen AFTER you've accomplished your goal. Don't watch yourself like an actor on a screen. Instead, look through your own eyes. Hear a loved one, or your boss or colleague congratulate you. Feel their palm as you shake it. Use your imaginary voice and mouth to say, "Thank you," in response. When you're waking up, before you even open your eyes, repeat that scene that would imply you have already achieved your goal. Before you get up to use the bathroom in the middle of the night, act out that scene again. Watch as you're magically driven to make your desires real.

You can be more productive. The onus is on you now. So give it all you've got. See where you wind up within the next year or two. You'll never want to be anything less than productive again. You can take that to the bank!

References

Clive Fullagar and E. Kevin Kelloway, "Work-Related Flow," in A Day in the Life of a Happy Worker, ed. Arnold B. Bakker and Kevin Daniels (New York: Psychology Press, 2013)

Christopher P. Neck and Charles C. Manz, Mastering Self-Leadership: Empowering Yourself for Personal Excellence, 6th ed. (Upper Saddle River, NJ: Pearson Prentice-Hall, 2012).

Daniel J. Levitin, "The Organized Mind: Thinking Straight in the Age of Information Overload" (New York: Dutton, 2014).

Francis Heylighen and Clément Vidal, "Getting Things Done: The Science Behind Stress-Free Productivity," Long Range Planning 41, no. 6 (2008)

F. Luthans, B. J. Avolio, J. B. Avey, and S. M. Norman, "Positive Psychological Capital: Measurement and Relationship with Performance and Satisfaction," Personnel Psychology 60, no. 3, (2007).

Mihaly Csikszentmihalyi, Flow: The Psychology of Optimal Experience (New York: Harper Perennial, 1990).

Mihaly Csikszentmihalyi and J. LeFevre, "Optimal Experience in Work and Leisure," Journal of Personality and Social Psychology 56, no. 5 (1989)

J. B. Avey, F. Luthans, R. M. Smith, and N. F. Palmer, "Impact of Positive Psychological Capital on Employee Well-being Over Time," Journal of Occupational Health Psychology 15, no. 1 (2010).

Peter M. Gollwitzer and Gabrielle Oettingen, "Planning Promotes Goal Striving," in Kathleen D. Vohs and Roy F. Baumeister, eds., Handbook of Self-Regulation: Research, Theory, and Applications, 2nd ed. (New York: Guilford, 2011).

Roy F. Baumeister and E. J. Masicampo, "Unfulfilled Goals Interfere with Tasks That Require Executive Functions," Journal of Experimental Social Psychology 47, no. 2 (2011)

Roy F. Baumeister and E. J. Masicampo, "Consider It Done! Plan Making Can Eliminate the Cognitive Effects of Unfulfilled Goals," Journal of Personality and Social Psychology 101, no. 4 (2011)

Roy F. Baumeister and John Tierney, Willpower: Discovering the Greatest Human Strength (New York: Penguin Press, 2011).

Schrager S, Sadowski E. Getting More Done: Strategies to Increase Scholarly Productivity. J Grad Med Educ. 2016

T. Sun, X. W. Zhao, L. B. Yang, and L. H. Fan, "The Impact of Psychological Capital on Job Embeddedness and Job Performance Among Nurses: A Structural Equation Approach," Journal of Advanced Nursing 68, no. 1 (2012)

www.ingramcontent.com/pod-product-compliance
Lightning Source LLC
Chambersburg PA
CBHW070048230426
43661CB00005B/815